CLASSICAL
ACTING

CLASSICAL
$\mathcal{A}$CTING

MALCOLM MORRISON

A & C Black · London
Heinemann · New Hampshire

For Johanna and Niki

First published 1995
A & C Black (Publishers) Limited
35 Bedford Row, London WC1R 4JH

ISBN 0-7136-4047-2

© 1995 Malcolm Morrison

First published in 1996 in the USA by Heinemann
A Division of Reed Elsevier, Inc.
361 Hanover Street, Portsmouth, NH 03801-3912
Offices and Agents throughout the world.

Distributed in Canada by Reed Books Canada
75 Clegg Road, Markham, Ontario L6G 1A1

ISBN 0-435-07019-3

CIP catalogue records for this book are available from
the British Library and the Library of Congress.

Cover photograph of RSC production of *The Country Wife*
taked by Clive Barda reproduced with permission of P.A.L.

Typeset in 10.5 by 12.5 pt Sabon Roman by Florencetype
Printed in Great Britain by Redwood Books, Trowbridge

Contents

Acknowledgements

The publishers would like to thank the following for giving their permission for the quotations listed. The publishers have employed their best endeavours to trace all copyright holders and apologise to any not listed.

Enthusiasms by Bernard Levin. Copyright © 1983 by Bernard Levin, reprinted by permission of Crown Publishers (USA) and Jonathan Cape, (UK).

Penguin Books Ltd for extracts from *Antigone* and *King Oedipus* from *The Theban Plays* by Sophocles translated by E.F. Watling and *Electra* and *Medea* from *Medea and Other Plays* by Euripedes translated by Philip Vellacot.

Weidenfeld and Nicolson for extract from *On Acting* by Laurence Olivier.

Amber Lane Press for extract from *Sir Donald Wolfit* by Ronald Harwood.

Introduction

What is a 'classical' play? The best definition that I can produce is: 'One which is highly structured, is representative of its time and author, deals with enduring themes, often expressed in heightened, literary language, has stood the test of time and is not related to colloquial and modern experiences.' Of course it would be much easier to give a list of playwrights whose work one believes to be 'classical'. Shakespeare, Molière, Sophocles, Shaw, Ibsen and Chekhov, though they wrote in very different styles and, indeed, for very different purposes, would all have to be included. This uneasiness in defining the exact parameters of 'classicism', while it is perplexing and frustrating, is somewhat relieved by the knowledge that amongst theatre practitioners there is a commonly shared body of dramatic literature which most would call 'classical'. In the examples used in this book I have called upon that common knowledge, since it is not my intention to propose a thesis of what classicism is, but rather to examine those plays and their time, style and content from the point of view of the actor.

In writing this book I have to face the uncomfortable fact that books on acting can never do justice to the topic and invariably fail to account for the heart of theatre which lies in human beings interacting with one another. This sharing of human experience accounts for satisfaction and continuing popularity of theatre since the earliest of times. Another factor is the sense of ritual, which is related both to the occasion and to the nature of the play itself. This coming together of a group of people in one place at an agreed time to engage in a phantasy and a mystery, where parts of the human condition and the stories about it will be re-enacted and examined, where our emotional responses as well as our speculative intellectual capacities will be exercised, is an act of the spirit. The theatre, like all the arts, educates our feelings. In viewing the follies and triumphs of other human beings in the safe environment of a theatre, we learn much about ourselves. The more we learn, even in a minor comedy, the more satisfied we are. The experience of the theatre is irreplaceable, and although television and film may present reality better than it can ever be produced upon a stage, they cannot make the same

1

spiritual appeal as the theatre, in which an audience which has willingly suspended disbelief quietly allows the actor to work upon its thoughts and feelings.

This places a huge responsibility upon the actor; he or she has charge of that audience and is responsible for using its time wisely and valuably. The audience should not be exploited or duped. The experience of a performance lies not only in the power and ingenuity of the text; it is also in the act of acting itself – the transformation and the elevation of human expectation in which the skill of the actor changes known circumstances into the unknown and makes disbelief belief.

What of these actors? Who is he or she? What must they do? What must they know? What do they bring to their art? How can they prepare for the responsibility which rests on them? In *The art of the theatre* Edward Gordon Craig, the stage designer and producer, said:

> The ideal actor will be the man who possesses both a rich nature and a powerful brain. Of his nature we need not speak. It will contain everything. Of his brain we can say that the finer the quality the less liberty will it allow itself, remembering how much depends upon its co-worker, the Emotion, and also the less liberty will it allow its fellow-worker, knowing how valuable to it is its sternest control. Finally, the intellect would bring both itself and the emotions to so fine a sense of reason that the work would never boil to the bubbling point with its restless exhibition of activity, but would create the perfect moderate heat which it would know how to keep temperate. The perfect actor would be he whose brain could conceive and could show us the perfect symbols of all which his nature contains. He would not ramp and rage up and down in Othello, rolling his eyes and clenching his hands in order to give us an impression of jealousy; he would tell his brain to inquire into the depths, to learn all that lies there, and then to remove itself to another sphere, the sphere of the imagination, and there fashion certain symbols which, without exhibiting the bare passions, would none the less tell us clearly about them.

This is one view. There are many more and it is not my intention in this book to define the perfect actor, realising that definition is impossible and that ultimately the way of acting is individual and personal; rather I wish to examine the apparent challenges to any actor and to offer a viewpoint and a resource in approaching those challenges.

This is an enormous subject, which deserves many volumes, books on sociology, anthropology, the physics of sound, social history, Greek, Latin, semiotics, textual criticism – but fortunately many have been written already. So, while acknowledging the need for background, I have tried to emphasise the practical art of the actor, with due respect to the need for information upon which to act. Since there are also many practical and worthwhile books on the subject of acting itself, I have mainly, but not exclusively, confined my references to plays written before the rise of modern realism in the theatre. We still see the results of Stanislavski's revolution in our theatre today, and the works of Ibsen and Chekhov and their successors are all the better for the new style of acting which it introduced. There is no need for me to interpret the work of Stanislavski or those great acting masters that followed; their opinions are available to read from the source. Instead I have tried to apply our modern sensibility and expectations – for we cannot ignore these influences – to the works of earlier writers and the challenges they present. It is not my intention to reconstruct earlier styles of acting. That would be impossible as well as pointless. We can only approach acting from what we know now. What can be said in a book is full of limitations, but if it helps to provoke thought and stimulate active pursuit of the craft, then it may be of some service.

The exercises in this book are all ones that I have used and which the actors I have worked with have found useful in some way. They are not the only way. There will never be one way.

1

Classical versus contemporary

THE MODERN ACTOR'S RESPONSIBILITIES

The way we look at a play now is not only affected by *individual* experience; it can also be affected by the passage of time, the accumulation of knowledge and changing fashion, which affect *everyone*. In many respects this is one of the greatest challenges facing the modern actor. While we wish to interpret the play and maintain fidelity with the author's intentions, the background that we have in the historical and social context may be at best cursory and at worst non-existent. Not only has our knowledge of facts changed and, in general, been enhanced; even the nature and purpose of theatre has changed over the centuries, and the factors that drew large crowds to the plays of Sophocles, Shakespeare and Shaw have changed. The solemn ritual and celebration which were central to the theatre in very early times have given way to the expectation of 'entertainment'. This need not necessarily reduce the importance of the event or the serious-ness with which a production is undertaken. There are common strands of human thought and feeling which unite the earliest experience with the most modern, and although the form of theatre may have changed, the examination of the human condition is still just as pressing and serious. In fact one is often surprised by the relevance today of viewpoints that are expressed in earlier plays.

The themes that appear in classical plays are common to being human in whatever age. Courtship, mistaken identity, honour, for example, are still as much at issue today as they were when any of the plays of Plautus, Shakespeare or Molière were holding their audiences. The challenge to the modern actor, therefore, is not primarily in discerning the themes of a play or in recognising what is human or true in any of them, but rather in the language and structure of the play itself and in the specifics which contribute towards the context in which the events are played out.

For example, our view of fairies today is very different from that of the average Elizabethan who watched *A Midsummer Night's Dream*. For us, fairy lore is a whimsical mythology that has more to do with romance than with the daily lives of people, whereas the average Elizabethan was well able to reconcile the existence of a mischievous but influential sub-culture with their deeper religious beliefs.

As another example, take the romance novels which Lydia Languish is furtively reading at the opening of *The Rivals*. They would certainly be very tame fare to modern readers because the gothic horrors which shocked readers in the eighteenth and nine-teenth centuries are now only so much melodrama to a society weaned on explicit violence. However, it is not difficult for an actor who understands the intent to make such a text playable by relating it to contemporary experience.

Our viewpoint of a play is often bounded by our specific knowledge of any given period, and this demands research. Certain references can easily lose their meaning over a period of time – or, indeed, their authenticity. This is probably as great a problem as any in the playing of classical roles. For example, if we look at an individual word like 'awful', the original meaning was 'awe inspiring' rather than the pejorative that it represents now. Then there are specific references to events, as in Hardcastle's speech in Act III, scene i of *She Stoops to Conquer*, where he says 'When I was in my best story of the Duke of Marlborough and Prince Eugene, he asked if I had not a good hand at making punch.' No doubt audiences of the day knew who these people were and what Mr Hardcastle is referring to – now it is the responsibility of the actor to find out. This loss of meaning is nowhere more apparent than in Shakespeare's comedies, where the topical humour has been lost. Look, for example, at the Latin lesson in *The Merry Wives of Windsor* Act IV, scene iii. At a time when Latin was taught as a required part of the school curriculum and was heard regularly in church, the scene would have made sense. Nowadays, in the absence of that background, it can seem irrelevant.

It is not only the meanings of words which change, but also the accepted mode of expression. For instance, in the world of Shakespeare, the idea of people arguing causes and interchanging ideas, one to one, in an alehouse was accepted. Language was not only a means to gain control over one's environment, or for the pursuit of commerce, it was also the currency of entertainment. It was not uncommon for young men to compose sonnets and throw them through the windows of their would-be paramours. Who could write a sonnet today? And who would go to the trouble of delivering it? Evenings of debate and discussion of news and ideas were common, and the way in which opinions were expressed was as important as the opinions themselves.

In the eighteenth century ideas and news were disseminated in coffee houses or at gatherings for an evening of music. In plays like *The School for Scandal*, notice how people gather to hear who has recently arrived in town or who has taken a mistress. Gentlemen swapped the latest information on a scientific discovery, discussed the political concerns of the day or lamented the latest happenings at Court. They drank chocolate and entertained each other with stories and theories, and the language they used was a vital sign of education and social standing.

The use of metaphor and simile was an accepted part of conversation in earlier centuries. An ordinary sailor once wrote to Queen Elizabeth I for a pay rise. He was a perfectly ordinary seaman sailing on one of Her Majesty's ships at a time when such a life was dangerous and England had just begun its discovery of the New World. Hygiene was unknown, and death came not only from the enemy but from the lack of sanitation on the ship. The sailor made his request and then ended his letter with this justification: 'For you see our lives are plumed with the feathers of death'. That the sailor wrote directly to his queen says much about the size of London at the time, which was probably about as populated as one of our modern medium-sized towns; it says much about the concept of monarchy and the role of monarchs in the day-to-day lives of their subjects (something to be considered when acting in the history plays of Shakespeare) and it says a great deal about the language which even the common person used. Before education became available for everyone, the ability to read and access to reading matter were largely confined to the clergy and scholars, and it was well into the nineteenth century before literacy was available to the majority. In general, people's experience of language came through stories read in church or plays performed at the play house. This was the literary experience of the majority.

Language was as subject to change and development as any scientific idea or political principle. Shakespeare brought words like 'obscene' and 'submerged' into the language for the first time. Bernard Levin wrote:

If you cannot understand my argument, and declare 'It's Greek to me', you are quoting Shakespeare; if you claim to be more sinned against than sinning, you are quoting Shakespeare; if you recall your salad days, you are quoting Shakespeare; if you act more in sorrow than in anger, if your wish is father to the thought, if your lost property has vanished into thin air, you are quoting Shakespeare; if you have ever refused to budge an inch or suffered from green-eyed jealousy, if you have played fast and loose, if you have been tongue tied, a tower of strength, hood-winked or in a pickle, if you have knitted your brows, made a virtue of necessity, insisted on fair play, slept not a wink, stood on ceremony, danced attendance (on your lord and master), laughed yourself into stitches, had short shrift, cold comfort or too much of a good thing, if you have seen better days or lived in a fool's paradise – why, be that as it may, the more fool you, for it is a foregone conclusion that you are (as good luck would have it) quoting Shakespeare; if you think it is early days and clear out bag and baggage, if you think it is high time and that that is the long and short of it, if you believe that the game is up and that truth will out even if it involves your own flesh and blood, if you lie low till the crack of doom because you suspect foul play, if you have your teeth set on edge (at one fell swoop) without rhyme or reason, then – to give the devil his due – if the truth were known (for surely you have a tongue in your head) you are quoting Shakespeare; even if you bid me good riddance and send me packing, if you wish I was dead as a door nail, if you think I am an eyesore, a laughing stock, the devil incarnate, a stony hearted villain, bloody-minded or a blinking idiot, then – by Jove! O Lord! Tut tut! for goodness' sake! what the dickens! but me no buts – it is all one to me, for you are quoting Shakespeare.

It is not only the question of semantics or social context which poses a challenge to a modern actor; there is the further question of expected behaviour. The ways in which people interact with each other socially change, as does what is deemed to be 'polite'; so does expected behaviour, which often explains why a scene takes the form that it does. We are a long way now from the days of books of 'Courtesy' which were current in medieval times and were perpetuated well into the nineteenth century. These books represented instruction in what was noble, what was expected of a lady or a gentlemen, and often gave very specific rules for every aspect of behaviour and belief. They had such extravagant titles as *Youth's Behaviour, or Decency in Conversation amongst Men* (published in 1640) or *An Essay to Revive the Ancient Education of Gentlewomen in Religion, Manners, Arts and Tongues, with an Answer to the Objections against this way of Education* (1673).

The effect of these rules can be seen everywhere in classical literature: to whom and how one accords deference, who is regarded as superior and what is considered appropriate and humane behaviour to people of a lower station. Accomplishments such as painting, writing or playing musical instruments were expected of people of 'quality', and from the earliest times the ability to dance was a major social necessity. As Joan Wildeblood and Peter Brinson say in their admirable book *The Polite World*, dancing meant 'the complete training in deportment and movement of the body'. This training in dance and deportment reached its absolute height in the eighteenth century, when dancing masters were to be seen at every aristocratic house, coaching the young people in every aspect of social appearance and tutoring the mature members of the household on the dances fashionable for that year. The inscription in a *Dancing Masters Pocket Book for the year 1805* reads 'Country Dances as to be performed at Court, Bath and all Public Assemblies'. It is 'Humbly dedicated to the Nobility and Gentry'.

Until comparatively recently, society was highly stratified, and everyone had a position to maintain. A great deal of the comedy of the seventeenth and eighteenth centuries is founded on this delineation of strata and the amusing attempts of one class of person to join another: witness Bob Acres in Act III of *The Rivals* learning to dance in order to join the aristocracy of the town, or Lady Bracknell in *The Importance of Being Earnest* laying down rules as to what constitutes eligibility for marriage.

All the foregoing is by way of articulating what I believe to be major responsibilities for the modern actor in preparing a role in any classical play. The examples and background are certainly not exhaustive, and every play makes its own individual demands.

SUMMARY

1. Examine and execute the form. That is: be capable of speaking verse, or handling a language that seems 'overblown' or literary.

2. Have an exact understanding of the content of the play. What does it say specifically? What do individual words and obscure references mean?

3. Research and appreciate the context of the events and behaviour in the play.

EXERCISES

1. Read as much as you can. Set yourself targets, like reading all the sonnets of Shakespeare, an exercise that reveals a great deal about the personality of the world's greatest playwright. Begin by reading all the plays mentioned in this book.

2. Keep notes on everything you read. It is an important part of an actor's armoury to have a knowledge of the classical repertoire, including a familiarity with roles for which he or she may be suitable.

3. Avoid the danger of reading only about theatre and plays. Expand your reading to develop your background and increase your knowledge of the conditions and times in which the plays were written.

4. Look at paintings and sculpture of the period.

5. Visit museums and see the artifacts from a certain period.

6. Go to the theatre.

2
Style and content

THE SEARCH FOR MEANING BEFORE MEANS

Sir Tyrone Guthrie, writing a foreword to a 1954 edition of plays by Richard Brinsley Sheridan, said:

> I have seen so many productions of Sheridan in which one could never come to terms with the characters because their impersonators were striking so many elegant attitudes, tapping snuff boxes, flourishing fans and delivering phrases, already well polished by Sheridan, with so much additional gloss that one was dazzled but neither interested or amused.

What is described here is the constant challenge to the actor to make the role seem comfortable, natural and appropriate, without overwhelming it with technical displays of superficial attitudinising or reckless exploitation of vocal or physical technique. The performances in classical plays that have satisfied me most were those where I have been unaware of the actor playing the role. Much of the success of a characterisation begins with the kind of homework the actor does and a willingness to prepare the role in the most self-effacing way, by searching out the identity of the character unsparingly and as scrupulously as possible. Those actors who have developed tricks, or love their own voices or are unwilling to undertake the research necessary to increase the authority of their performance are likely to present something self-centred and self-conscious, just as Guthrie describes, where the superficial trappings of performance outweigh the essential human truths.

Too often in classical plays there is a temptation to be lulled or seduced by the words themselves. Many times I have stopped an actor or a student and asked, 'What does that mean', only to be told that they are not sure. Of course, it is not possible to understand everything immediately, that is the purpose of rehearsal and study. It is at the very beginning that it is most important to bear in mind that decisions should be related to the play itself, not to the actor playing the role. One should be more aware of what one is doing rather than how one is doing it. Technique should always be a support to the creative and intellectual search for a character, not a substitute.

When one is faced with the beauty of a phrase in a Greek play or in Shakespeare, its delivery must be informed by the meaning rather than the mere juxtaposition of evocative and musically satisfying words. It is too easy for the actor to make an immediate response to the text, because what he reads affects him at various levels, mainly emotional, and so the meaning of the phrase in its context is overlooked and overwhelmed by a response to the beauty of it. For example there is something very attractive to an actor in saying, as Macbeth does, 'tomorrow, and tomorrow, and tomorrow / Creeps in this petty pace from day to day / To the last syllable of recorded time' (V.v.18–20). The further danger is that it was written by William Shakespeare and so demands a certain resonance in its delivery. What is certain is that the phrase and the ensuing argument, as well as the circumstances in which it is said, need to be examined in detail, for the point of the speech is not a beautiful musical experience, in which the actor can wax 'poetic', but rather a deep and intricate reflection on the part of a despairing thane, who has been taken to the limit of his resources and is at the end of one of the most harrowing personal journeys ever written about. Never take any moment for granted or be guilty of generalisations about the style of a play, because style can only be related to content.

One of the major problems in playing the classics is the 'generic' approach, where if one looked at an entire cast and changed the roles around, nothing conspicuously different would happen to the interpretation or execution of the play. The performances, grounded more in assumptions than in specific meanings, become devoid of personality and, for example, Lysander and Demetrius are merely generic 'young men': personable, vocally in the same range, of equal energy and devoted to their speeches more than they are to the women they are chasing. There is almost a standard physical stance for the actors, so that as soon as they begin to rehearse Shakespeare they ground themselves with feet apart, torso slightly thrust forward, hands on hips and a very earnest look. Or in an eighteenth-century play everyone speaks very quickly in a voice at least half an octave higher than normal, all the while holding arms uncomfortably in balletic positions and standing in fourth position. Yet everything in the text points to something quite different, and it is clearly the playwright's intent to define each of the characters. Helena and Hermia in *A Midsummer Night's Dream* are opposites in temperament, and Shakespeare is at pains to emphasise the contrasts, even in their physical height. Marlowe and Hastings in *She Stoops to Conquer* are not these 'generic' eighteenth-century young men, who have a lot of ballet training but no minds. They are contrasts to one another – one easy, assured, garrulous and active; the other quiet, gentle and retiring. I believe that to seek out these contrasts is a very good way to begin discovering and developing a role.

While the temptation to exhibit one's technique is great, there is another equal danger. That is to believe that technique is not necessary, that any vocal accomplishment and physical prowess is actually a betrayal of truth on the stage, that if it feels right then it must be right. This can lead, among other problems, to a lack of control which can actually imperil other actors on a stage – if, for example, you handle a sword when you have no technique or ability to do so. You may not have the vocal equipment to be heard; you may have inadequate diction and lack the ability to speak the form of the verse or the capacity to sustain and repeat a performance. The first duty of an actor is to be present, the second is to be heard and the third is to play the role reliably. One can have the grandest ideas in the world, but unless they are made manifest and performed with artistry they are of no value whatsoever. An idea is no good in and of itself; the theatre demands that it be made apparent. Sometimes this requires artifice as well as art – in other words it requires technique. The responsibility and talent of actors is to make an audience believe that they are witnessing private and intimate events, even though they are in a public space. This requires not only the actor's belief in his or her character and the situation, but a technical capacity to deal with all the pressures of performance in public.

A danger in acquiring technique is that it is not repeated often enough to become easy and discreet. I have seen many actors who are limited by their own vocal capacity, for example, and so the instrument limits what they can offer as a character. Poor breath control can easily diminish the actor's ability to phrase in classical plays, and so comedy can be lost in the plays of Shaw or Wilde because the actor cannot speak the long sense groups which the playwright has written. Some of the oratorical builds that are such a distinct dramatic device of Shakespeare can be lost because of lack of breath capacity. Take, for example, the following from *Julius Caesar*:

ANTONY

> A curse shall light upon the limbs of men;
> Domestic fury and fierce civil strife
> Shall cumber all the parts of Italy;
> Blood and destruction shall be so in use,
> And dreadful objects so familiar,
> That mothers shall but smile when they behold
> Their infants quartered with the hands of war,
> All pity choked with custom of fell deeds;
> And Caesar's spirit, ranging for revenge,
> With Ate by his side come hot from hell,
> Shall in these confines with a monarch's voice
> Cry 'havoc!' and let slip the dogs of war,
> That this foul deed shall smell above the earth
> With carrion men, groaning for burial.

(III.i.265–78)

If this is broken into one-line phrases rather than accumulating in intensity line by line, without long pauses for breaths, it is diminished. The drama and power of Marc Antony as a passionate and powerful orator is lost. We know less of Antony, and we have lost an opportunity to let the form assist the sense.

SUMMARY

1. It is important to create the basis for a character in specific enquiry and imaginative speculation.

2. Do not jump to early conclusions because of the effect the reading of the play has on *you*.

3. Resist generic assumptions about a character because of preconceptions and generalisations about style.

4. Develop technique which is consummate and easy and allows the freedom of creation.

5. At all times focus on what you are doing, rather than how you are doing it.

14

EXERCISES

1. Define very specifically for yourself what you believe the responsibilities of an actor are, then assess honestly how far you measure up to them. What do you avoid? What do you find onerous or make excuses to yourself about?

2. Pick a speech which you might use at an audition and begin work on it. Make sure you read the whole play. Assimilate the context thoroughly, focusing on the revelation of the character and what is happening. Avoid treating the speech as an independent show-piece for your technical skills or other attributes.

3. If you are not working on a role immediately, choose one which you would like to play. Begin work on that role by reading a chapter of this book and then going back to the study of the role and testing some of the advice which is given. Do not skip anything because it does not have immediate application. Remember that there are roles upon which one can work for a lifetime. You should begin your study early to play a Lear or a Queen Margaret. Most of the classics offer roles that require maturity of thought, and you are not only training yourself for that particular role, you are contributing to your fund of experience for every role you play.

3

Reading the text

STORY, BACKGROUND AND CHARACTERS

It is amazing that we are still reading and performing plays which are hundreds of years old. This is not just because they are interesting as documents of theatre history, artifacts of bygone ages and civilisations, but rather because they still have something very important to say today, which has meaning and validity in our social context. The theatre, like all art, has a role in educating our emotions, and those emotions have been common in man since time immemorial. We know that feelings of love and anger, jealousy and joy are basic to mankind – it is only what stimulates those feelings and the ways in which we express them that change their form. For example, the audience crammed into the 'wooden O' watching a performance of *Henry V* is engaged by an exhilarating tale of patriotism and heroics which might be comparable to the feelings when the football team you support narrowly wins a crucial match.

Theatre has traditionally been a place of influence, where emotions are excited and the intellect stimulated. In *Richard III* we watch a fascinating story, full of archetypes of good and evil, and enjoy that experience in safety. We listen to language of influence, taking into account not only the political arguments but also the emotional context, on the nature of excess and pride, and leave the theatre not only stimulated by having watched an exciting event, but also with our experience enhanced.

With this in mind, it is imperative that the play be understood profoundly by the actor and that the representation of it takes into account the narrative, the argument, the emotional context and the characters. Much of this is established in reading the play itself. Reading the play is the foundation of all the work that the actor will do. Shortcomings and misunderstandings at this stage of preparation will have their effect on the entire development of the work right up to and including performance. Profound understanding of the play allows the work to find focus, meaning and truth. This requires considerable personal discipline and a great deal of hard work.

There is often a temptation to accept the emotional under-standing of a certain scene without acknowledging the context. In *Romeo and Juliet*, for example, I have seen many actors do this in the famous garden scene, where Romeo woos Juliet from below her balcony. The presentation has certainly been passionate, even beautiful, but it lacks the tension that Shakespeare has built into the situation: at any moment the lovers may be discovered. Juliet's father has declared his intention to have Juliet marry Paris, and thus it would be a disaster (and a very quick ending to the play!) if Romeo were discovered in the Capulets' garden. The constant alternation between awareness of their situation and their flights of ecstasy, when their feelings overwhelm their circumstances and caution is thrown away, makes for a very important suspenseful dynamic in the scene. It gives the actor a clue to the tempo in which the scene should be played; it gives a context of danger which makes the event more reckless and urgent. It is this lack of time which urges the lovers to a hasty, impulsive commitment and sets the tone of irrevocable calamity which ensues and which is inevitable once it has been set in motion. The lovers do not have all the time in the world to wax lyrical in the balcony scene, and so their language is not the language of considered thought, but that of immediacy, and the poetry is symptomatic of their intensity.

It is improbable that at first reading you will understand the text completely; the language will feel unfamiliar, references will be elusive, even remembering who all the characters are can be taxing. But even the most astute scholar has to spend consider-able time looking at a play to understand it. The nearer we approach to our contemporary world the easier it seems to become. While it is often easy to understand what is taking place (the event), it may not be immediately clear why people are involved in it.

For example, in *Antigone* by Sophocles, we see Creon, the king, arguing with his son Haemon. It is very clear that they are opposed to one another, but the underlying love and the primal feelings of father for son also have to be recognised. The most important thing on this first reading is not to be daunted, and to continue reading even if every little nuance is not understood. Nor should you panic. There is a tendency, because of the bewil-dering amount of information to be absorbed, to believe that you

will never understand it. Do not let boredom or impatience overcome you. Some of the plays in the classic repertoire are so
unyielding at first reading that they can become boring. Only
when they are more deeply understood can they be stimulating.

I remember first reading *Electra* without having any notion of
the role of the chorus in the play, or traditionally within the form
of Greek theatre. So I ignored them. When I saw a long passage
on the page labelled 'Chorus' I would skip over it to get to the meat
of what the characters were doing. Only later, after learning that
the chorus is a commentator, the representative of the common
person, did I see the relevance and power of their contribution to
the drama, in which they perform an essential role rather than
merely punctuating the action. Try to read for the first time in a
very relaxed way and glean whatever you can. There is no require-
ment to understand everything at once. Indeed what then would
be the point of rehearsals? Remember rehearsals are not only
intended to consolidate what you are doing; they are also a time
of discovery, a time to explore meaning and feeling.

I have seen actors who use their reading and pre-rehearsal
preparation as full planning sessions, in which they determine
how things should be spoken and what everything is about.
They come to the first rehearsal with a series of privately held
opinions and predeterminations of how a scene will go, only
to be surprised that there are other actors in the scene who do
not see everything as they do. It is a very grave danger to be so
analytical and categorical. It can be very disconcerting to other
actors and can waste a lot of time if the actor has to be disabused
of an idea or a decision made too early in the process. Any system
of reading and preparation which is predicated on technical
assumptions is likely to lead to early and shallow interpretation of
the role. One test that the actor can apply during reading is 'Am I
reading this to find out about the play or the character, or am
I reading it to determine how I do it?' If you are reading to make
premature decisions on how it is done, then you are probably
missing a great many clues which will lead to full understanding
of the content of the play.

It should go without saying that you must read the whole play,
not just the scenes you are in. This should also be true throughout
the rehearsal process, because this is a very important part of
developing the sense of context in which one is acting. Many

things are said and established in one scene which have a bearing on subsequent or preceding scenes.

After reading the play for the first time you will find it useful to write very brief notes, outlining the story as much as you can and giving your first impressions of the characters. Remember it is not a literature examination, so there is no right or wrong: these are your very personal impressions and will give you a basis for further reading. So, just give your most natural and instinctive reactions, no matter how naive or ill-digested they may feel. This can be done very economically – just a few words, not a long essay. As far as the characters are concerned, write a few adjectives against their names that define your first impressions. These may, and probably will, change. Certainly as you continue your preparation they will become much more specific. However, these early reactions will help you to approach the play again with a more focused viewpoint. Bearing in mind that your initial reaction to Iago is 'evil, scheming, treacherous', for example, may cause you to go a stage further in the next reading to discover why he is so and exactly how subtle and plausible he is in his scenes with Othello. Tanner's apparent 'arrogance' in *Man and Superman* by George Bernard Shaw, or Harpagon's 'miserliness' in *The Miser* by Molière can expand into much fuller characterisations, with specific reasons why they are that way. On further reading you will also discover that they are not exclusively 'evil' or 'arrogant' or 'miserly'. These first assumptions on early reading of the play will probably be very broad generalisations, but they are the first step to achieving subtlety and a three-dimensional approach to the characters and the story.

For a second reading of the play have a dictionary near at hand. It is also useful to have a classical dictionary, in case of references to people and places in Greek and Roman Mythology, which occur frequently in classical texts. It is not a bad idea to know who the major Greek and Roman gods and goddesses are, and to know the names and areas of concern of the Nine Muses and the Fates in Greek mythology, since it is a given that you will come across them, even in eighteenth- and nineteenth-century plays (see Appendix 1). In a play like *The Rivals*, not only does Mrs Malaprop refer to them on occasion; she also gets them wrong. The actor playing Mrs Malaprop should know this. Armed with your dictionaries, read the play again and make a note of the words and references you do not understand. As you go or at the end of each scene look them up and make notes for yourself. There is no easy or short substitute for this. This is when you have to be meticulous and just slog at it. It is quite surprising how much one learns and how many new words can be added to your vocabulary. One consolation is that the more experience one has with classical plays, the easier it gets. Remember that this knowledge is a resource, not a weapon; do not allow yourself to become a know-it-all in rehearsal. Certainly there is every virtue in sharing information that can be of assistance to another actor, but there is also a grave danger that you can earn an uneasy reputation by parading the fruits of your research at every unasked-for opportunity. The research is intended to be something to act on, not to lecture about. As an exercise, try Hamlet's most famous speech 'To be, or not to be' (IV.i.58–). It is rewarding and revealing to discover the meaning of 'fardels' or 'a bare bodkin'.

In many editions of classical works you will find explanatory footnotes. They can certainly be very useful, but do not be deceived into thinking that they tell the whole story or that they can replace any work you may need to do for your own preparation. Remember, you cannot act footnotes. Some of the lengthier explanations have literary relevance and hypothetical interest for scholars, but they cannot be put on stage. The purpose of the actor's research and preparation is to find meaning and understanding so that decisions can be made. These form the basis of decisions in interpretation. In literary criticism the scholar has the luxury of saying 'either/or'; several possibilities can be investigated and the choice of one idea over another can rest with the reader. In the case of the actor, there must be a commitment to a particular choice of meaning. An actor cannot play a scene and then at the end of it say 'or' and do the scene again with another view point. The essence of any satisfactory research, rehearsal and performance is that choices have been investigated, agreements have been made and commitments are refined and executed. This is what interpretation means in practical terms. It is the distinctly personal viewpoints of the director, designers and actors, all collaborating on well-founded decisions, which make for the most interesting theatre.

After a couple of readings in which the general sense of the play and its characters has been established, as well as the specific meanings of words and references, begin to focus subsequent study on your character in the play. One very useful exercise in this third reading is to note what other people say about you. This is not necessarily true, but it is worth noting that others think that way, and it gives you a basis for considering how your character appears to others. In *Julius Caesar* (I.ii.195–6) Caesar says that Cassius 'has a lean and hungry look . . . Such men are dangerous', or later (V.v.67) Marc Antony says that Brutus 'was the noblest Roman of them all'. In *The Rivals*, Act I, Lydia says, 'Well, Julia, you are your own mistress (though under the protection of Sir Anthony), yet have you, for this long year been a slave to the caprice, the whim, the jealousy of this ungrateful Faulkland, who will ever delay assuming the right of a husband, while you suffer him to be equally imperious as a lover'. In *She Stoops to Conquer*, Act II, Mrs Hardcastle says to Tony, 'I never see you when you're in spirits. No, Tony, you then go to the alehouse or the kennel.' Many questions are raised for the actor and many obligations incurred as a result of such comments. The idea of Lydia being a 'slave' to love, the indecision and ingratitude of Faulkland in delaying a proposal to Lydia – these are matters that the actor playing those roles should carefully consider. Are the accusations true? If so, what do we see of those character traits in a performance and what form do they take? In *Julius Caesar*, how does an actor justify the opinion that he is the noblest Roman? Is there any necessity to do so? Is it true? What is nobility? And so the questions go on and can produce interesting and sometimes surprising answers, all of which can contribute to the building of the characterisation.

On a fourth or subsequent reading a very useful exercise is to create a graph of who meets whom and when. Try writing the characters' names down the left-hand side of the paper and divide the rest of the page into columns for the various scenes. Go through the play and mark your graph when a character is in the scene. At the conclusion of your reading review the graph, and it will tell you who meets whom, and when. This is very important information. One of the most important parts of developing a role is to play the changes that a character goes through. It is vital to the structure of the play and the fulfilment of the emotional growth in a characterisation. After all, if any character is the same at the end of a play, or indeed, a scene, as he or she was at the beginning, it is likely to be a fairly boring evening in the theatre. So much of what we witness as an audience is related to how the characters learn and change, how much and in what way they react to the circumstances presented in the play. The increasing desperation of Macbeth, the piling on of tragedy and the intensifying of event after event, each revealing more desperate action on his part, are the fibre of the play. The actor who struts onto the stage and leaves at the end with as much bombast has missed the point. Try taking it scene by scene and ask yourself, 'How did he change?' The Macbeth that goes out to murder King Duncan is changed by doing it. When he returns to the stage he is drained and horrified and has faced a critical circumstance in his life that will not allow him to be the same confident soldier we saw at the beginning who earned praise and titles from his king. We need to detail those changes because they and the transitions between them are the vital underpinning to structure in a performance.

This may seem to be a very large amount of preparation; it may even feel unnecessary, but can one really be too well prepared? It is certainly preferable to cursory knowledge of the play, inadequate understanding of the language and ignorance of the references or historical circumstances. The nature of this work should be liberating. It allows many more choices for the actor in rehearsal; it gives an authority to his or her choices and ultimately greater satisfaction with the result.

A word of caution is needed here about small roles. It is frequently said that there are no small parts, only small actors. While it is true that being cast in a minimal role is sometimes unsatisfying and that there may not be as much to learn in doing them, it is also clear that once having been allocated the responsibility of making the announcement 'The carriage awaits, my Lord', the actor should develop a character and offer the best in terms of relevant creative choice. One should never succumb to the very tempting danger of believing that one's role is unimportant or purely functional. This kind of attitude can lead to casualness and indifference, which should never be part of any rehearsal or performance. I once saw a performance descend from major tragedy to outright farce on the arrival of an inept messenger, whose tabard was tucked into the back of his tights, proclaiming the death of the queen (or some important character) in high, lisping tones, without any connection to the play or the role that he was playing.

Always beware of sweeping assumptions and the view that every herald and messenger, every butler and maid is the same stock character. Look at Mountjoy in *Henry V*. He is certainly the messenger on behalf of the French, but he has a very defined personality which impresses King Henry. The roles of the butlers Merriman and Lane in *The Importance of Being Earnest*, are real gems. Look at the wryness, the affection and the occasional insolence of Lane in dealing with Algernon's capriciousness. The fact that, after he has been put on the spot by Algernon in front of Lady Bracknell, he says that there were no cucumbers to be had 'even for ready money' speaks volumes about his personality and his relationship with his employer. It is a very rewarding role, even though he appears only in Act I.

Everyone on the stage must be a personality, with distinct objectives, and though you may have been given very few clues in the text in terms of what is said directly about your presence, with a little thought, some imagination and a close understanding of the text, it is possible to invest even the smallest character with personality and life.

Nothing you do in this early preparation should be final. You have only examined the facts. You have not established all that will be necessary for the ultimate interpretation of the role or the play. That, of course, will be left to the negotiation which takes place in a rehearsal between the director and you. All you have done is to develop a readiness for the next stage of the production.

SUMMARY

1. Read the play thoroughly. Do not try to achieve complete understanding from a cursory initial reading.

2 Look at the development of the play and the character. Look for the changes in the character.

3. Look up the meanings of words and references.

4. Remember that this is not the time to determine how you will perform the role; it is only a preparation for the choices you will make later.

5. The actor has a responsibility to the whole play, no matter how small the role may be.

6. Never use research as a defence against challenge and daring with your choices. Your increased comprehension of the text is intended to support and underpin your imagination and creativity.

EXERCISES

1. Choose a play and a role and read it. Jot down the words you do not understand. Look them up at the end of each scene, or as they occur; the word may recur and there is no point in continuing to read without understanding. Remember you can also use a classical dictionary, which will give you more information on the Greek and Roman legends.

2. Make yourself a character graph. Write the names of all the characters in a column down the left-hand side of the page. Then square off the rest of the page for the number of acts and scenes in the play. If the scenes are long, as in nineteenth-century plays, use page numbers – say every ten pages. As you read the play and a character appears, make a mark in the appropriate square.

3. Note when your character appears and with whom he or she meets. Note carefully what happens in the scene, particularly what is revealed about your character which is new. What changes take place in the scene? What does your character discover in the scene which was previously unknown? Ask yourself how your presence furthers the story.

4. Ask yourself if your character behaves consistently and predictably. Note carefully any inconsistencies.

5. Is your character telling the truth, or are you practising any kind of deception? Why? And when is the truth revealed?

6. Read the play again, and this time make a note of what other characters say about you. Assess whether you believe the statement to be true or false. Remember that sometimes another character is trying to build a profile of you which is not accurate. Why? And when is the truth acknowledged or revealed?

7. If you accept a statement as true, ask yourself where in the play this can be shown.

8. Review the scenes you are in and give yourself one or two words that define the emotional state of your character at the beginning of the scene and one or two words for his or her state at the end of the scene. Be aware that you must portray the transition from one to the other.

4

Narrative and atmosphere

WHAT, WHY AND HOW

This is one of the most difficult subjects in acting the classics. The effective balance between the story and the heightened images which express it is very difficult to achieve – and to write about.

Firstly, what do we mean by 'narrative'? The easy answer is, of course, the story – the series of events leading towards a conclusion which resolves some of the issues and circumstances in the play. It is the portrayal of events by which we understand that something has happened. If we take a simple story like *Little Red Riding Hood*, the stress is on the narrative when we describe the events which took place. Red Riding Hood goes to her grand-mother's house. She meets a wolf on the way. The wolf dashes off to grandmother's house, takes grandmother from her bed and hides her in a closet. The wolf then dresses in grandmother's clothes and takes her place in bed. Red Riding Hood arrives at grandmother's house . . . and so on. These are the bare bones of the story, and although the events described are faithful to the story they contain only the facts. They do not give any hint of the reasons why one tells it, only what takes place. This account gives no indication of any emotional progress or philosophical concern. It is the road map, but it in no way represents the land-scape and the experiences that are to be had when the real journey is undertaken. Of course, it is absolutely necessary to understand the sequence of events and to be able to develop the other content in the play as a result of this very basic story. It can also provide an important discipline for the actor's creativity. For example, the plot of a commedia dell'arte play can be highly complex. In developing the possibilities of character it can be very easy to lose sight of the central story, so that the improvisation and develop-ment of the characters overwhelms the story-telling. At some time in rehearsal it will probably be necessary to review the business which has developed as part of character development and make sure that the narrative is still clearly delineated. Otherwise it will be a play about actors being funny characters without a clear sense of the story on which all the business depends. But this is also true when *what* the actor is doing becomes more important than *why* he or she is doing it.

Once the story is truly appreciated, the next step is to examine why the events take place. This is important in discovering the characters and the emotional content of the play. In understanding the reaction to a narrative event the nature of the characters has to be considered. When Orestes returns and Electra meets him again, or when the Princess of France in *Love's Labour's Lost* postpones the meeting of the lovers for a year, that is what they do, but in order to act these critical moments of the narrative there has to be a reason for their doing so. Sometimes this is not articulated in the text. Even if a character says why they are doing something it need not necessarily be true. The actor has to establish the true reasons and then decide whether they are revealed or hidden.

Looking for the clues as to why things happen can sometimes be easier in classical plays, since the playwright will often provide the reason. This is something an actor with our contemporary sensibility has to get used to. It is highly unlikely that the playwright of today would write such blatant motivation as is contained in a work by Shakespeare, for example. Look at the soliloquy of Richard, who is still Duke of Gloucester, before he becomes Richard III (at the very beginning of that play). He lays out very clearly what kind of person he is and why he will do what he does within the play:

> I that am rudely stamped and want love's majesty
> To strut before a wanton ambling nymph,
> I that am curtailed of this fair proportion,
> Cheated of feature by dissembling nature.
> Deformed, unfinished, sent before my time
> Into this breathing world scarce half made up –
> And that so lamely and unfashionable
> That dogs bark at me as I halt by them –
> Why, I in this weak piping time of peace
> Have no delight to pass away the time,
> Unless to spy my shadow in the sun
> And descant on mine own deformity.
> And therefore since I cannot prove a lover
> To entertain these fair well-spoken days,
> I am determined to prove a villain
> And hate the idle pleasures of these days.

(I.i.16–31)

Here he clarifies the reasons why the narrative will unfold as it does; in fact he articulates his own motivation. This can occasionally be uncomfortable for the modern actor. We live in a post-Freudian world; we have grown comfortable with analysis and have some understanding of the layering of human behaviour, so we look for a more subtle kind of acting and expect to understand the reasons for human behaviour by indirect means as well as by what is overt. Consequently, we are a little wary of direct statement of motivation. It helps a great deal to accept that many characters in the classical plays before, say, Ibsen and Chekhov, are only *saying* what many of our modern characters may be *thinking*. The purpose of Hamlet's famous soliloquies is to reveal the private workings of his thought and feelings. We learn in some depth how he is dealing with his situation, the thoughts and memories that have been stirred and, further, we learn of his intentions. It is important in most of the classical repertoire to examine the text scrupulously to find the reason for the behaviour of a character. It can be quite simple. I have seen actors who want to complicate the story by overloading it with pseudo-psychological reasoning, when in fact the reason for the character's behaviour is clearly and directly stated in the text. It is our modern tendency, if we are not careful, to mistrust the simplicity of the author's statement in favour of more complex theory. This is not to say that our understanding of human behaviour is wrong, merely that we must try to find the reasons in the text itself before overlaying them with complicated and unplayable theories. The actions which a person takes and the reasons for that action have to be manifest and playable within a scene; we cannot provide footnotes in the programme explaining a simple moment with extended theoretical justification. Remember that many of the plays in the classical repertoire were written at a time when people believed that what you are as a person and what you do as a person were the same thing.

In addition to discerning what is happening and why, and the reasons for a character's behaviour, it is important to examine the nature of the language which is used. The kind of language and the imagery contribute greatly to the feeling and experience associated with the circumstances. It is a danger to invest too much in the images without the underlying support of the narrative. Here I speak of the kind of performance where the actor is so engaged with relishing the images and the sounds that the sense and vitality of the story are lost. A character who begins with imagery, like Tieresias in Sophocles, *Antigone*, with 'E'er the chariot of the sun has rounded once or twice his wheeling way', is clearly in an elevated state of emotion, well beyond the common experience. It also suggests the awesomeness of what is to follow. Who is this person capable of majestic, elevated thought? He is the one who is about to prophesy the result of Creon's actions and make predictions of greater tragedy to follow. He is blind, and yet he is a 'seer'. He tells a story in the ensuing speech, but the manner in which it is conveyed has a universal and dreadful importance to all in the play and all who observe it. The actor has to learn to manage both the narrative and the imagery with which it is described. It cannot all be 'poetry'. Clearly the poetry must embody and reflect an intense intent. To avoid the problem of wallowing in the poetry, the actor should always keep in mind what the objective is in saying what he does.

The following speech from *The Rivals* Act III, scene iii is another good example of images serving the narrative. It describes Absolute's restlessness in love. It is not sentimental or reflective. The character is very active and energetic, and although he is talking about love there is a vigour and strength in the images that complement the sense:

> Ah! my soul. What a life will we then live! Love shall be our idol and support! we will worship him with a monastic strictness: abjuring all worldly toys, to centre every thought and action there. Proud of calamity, we will enjoy the wreck of wealth; while the surrounding gloom of adversity shall make the flame of our pure love show doubly bright.

Once you have considered what takes place and why, it is appropriate to look at how the playwright expresses the thoughts and feelings of the character. This has very much to do with the personal style of the playwright and the individual interpretation of the actor. At a literary level what something means can be fairly well established and agreed by a reasonably intelligent reader; the power and talent of the actor lies in the ability to take these facts and by recognising the imagery, the resonances of thought and feeling underlying the actual events, to present a character who is plausibly engaged in those events. Theatre is not a finite pursuit, where if one creates the right equation of meaning and feeling the result is inevitable. Theatre relies upon the personal investment and individual creative responses of each actor to present a fresh and revealing interpretation of the role and the play. One of the beauties of all great plays is that they can be seen many times, and that every interpretation of the same blueprint presents a different viewpoint. There is no way of achieving a definitive presentation of any great play. It is this area of the theatre art which leads to the greatest triumphs and disasters. This is very well expressed in a review which appeared in *The Tatler* in 1831 of William Charles Macready's Macbeth by the writer and critic Leigh Hunt. Note that the opinion rests on the failure of the actor's imaginative response to the imagery.

> Macbeth was performed here [Drury Lane] last night – the principal character by Mr. Macready; Lady Macbeth by Miss Huddart. We are loth to find fault with one who gives so much pleasure as Mr. Macready; but his Macbeth is not one of his most effective performances. It wants the poetry of the original; that is to say, *it wants in its general style and aspect that grace and exaltation which is to the character what the poetry is to the language; which, in fact is the poetry of the tragedy;* and which, without depriving it of its nature enables the tragic criminal to move fitly in the supernatural sphere of his error. In other words, the passion of Mr. Macready's Macbeth wants imagination.

The italics are mine. Hunt then goes on to express perfectly what I would wish to say regarding the questions of 'What? Why? and How?':

> Mr. Macready seems afraid of the poetry of some of his greatest parts, as if it would hurt the effect of his naturalness and his more familiar passages: but such a fear is not a help towards nature; it is only an impulse towards avoiding a difficulty. The highest union of the imaginative with the passive is the highest triumph of acting, as it is of writing.

SUMMARY

1. Know clearly what takes place. Establish the narrative, not only of the play but for your character. What is his or her complete story within the play?

2. Learn why the character behaves that way. Remember that it can be a danger to develop reasons that are too complex to act.

3. Study the language and images the character uses.

4. Remember that avoiding the poetry and the heightened expression of thought is to ignore the style and much of the challenge of acting in a classical play.

EXERCISES

1. Choose an extended speech from a classical play – the messenger in a Greek play is a good choice – and read the speech identifying and stressing all the verbs. Gather the purpose and energy and sense of the narrative from this reading.

2. Read it again without the excessive stress but try to maintain your focus on the story, irrespective of the atmosphere and emotional state of the character. Note particularly where the story advances; where something else is learned. Do this like a totally dispassionate news reader, who conveys even the most grievous news without emotional engagement.

3. Read again, this time stressing the adjectives and adverbs. Observe the quality of the words and respond to them with your voice. Note the juxtaposition of sounds and how they contribute.

4. Knowing the context of the speech and the story, speak the speech again conveying the story and the emotional state of the character.

5

Words, words, words

SPEAKING AND LISTENING

In today's world there is an emphasis on speedy, ready communication, so that a language trading mainly in verbs, nouns and pronouns has emerged. Sometimes even a grunt will suffice as adequate communication. Yet most of the material written by the classical playwrights not only conveys facts but also describes circumstances and feelings, and their use of adverbs and adjectives creates atmosphere and may also indicate the education and breeding of the speaker.

The words that we speak have a resonance of meaning well beyond their simple dictionary meaning. Take for example the speech of the Ghost of Hamlet's father: 'I am thy father's spirit.' Doomed for a certain term to walk the night.' (I.v.9–10). Note the use of the word 'spirit'. Think of all the words similar to 'spirit' and try to replace it: 'I am thy father's ghost . . .', 'I am thy father's spectre . . .', 'I am thy father's shade . . .', 'I am thy father's ghoul . . .'. They simply do not have the same impact. While they may correspond in literal meaning with the description in the Oxford Dictionary of 'spirit' meaning 'a disembodied or incorporeal being', they carry with them none of the associations that that word bears. This single word is so telling within the context of the scene because it not only tells Hamlet the identity of the being in front of him but implies that it is not just an 'incorporeal being' but is an embodiment of all his father's qualities, so that this presence is not only mysterious but mystical.

In all the ages represented in the classical literature it was considered a sign of grace and good manners, as well as education, to speak elegant sentences, with a fine mastery of vocabulary. The manner in which something was said was just as important as what was said. Language and declamation were very high on the list of what was considered appropriate in an education. Consider what Mrs Malaprop says in *The Rivals* of her expectations of a well-bred young lady:

I would by no means wish a daughter of mine to be a progeny of learning; I don't think so much learning becomes a young woman: for instance, I would never let her meddle with Greek, or Hebrew, or algebra, or simony, or fluxions, or paradoxes, or such inflammatory branches of learning – neither would it be necessary for her to handle any of your mathematical, astronomical, diabolical instruments. – But, Sir Anthony, I would send her, at nine years old, to a boarding school, in order to learn a little ingenuity and artifice. Then, sir, she should have a supercilious knowledge in accounts; – and as she grew up. I would have her instructed in geometry, that she might know something of the contagious countries; – but above all, Sir Anthony, she should be mistress of orthodoxy, that she might not mis-spell, and mis-pronounce words so shamefully as girls usually do; and likewise that she might reprehend the true meaning of what she is saying. This, Sir Anthony, is what I would have a woman know; – and I don't think there is a superstitious article in it.

The logical presumption was that if you were expected to speak in complete sentences and debate and discuss with clarity and logic, you were also expected to listen to a complete sentence. It was considered bad manners to interrupt. By contrast, listen to any conversation today and observe the interruptions, or note how few sentences are completed. One of the most difficult things for a modern actor is to feel comfortable speaking in complete and extended sentences, with metaphors, similes and images. We are not conditioned to it. It is also very difficult for an actor to stand and listen to someone else speaking in this way on stage. It requires a re-education of our listening habits and an attitude of mind in which the experience of conversation is as important as the actual message. So much of what is written in classical literature is capable of condensation and paraphrase, so that the essential message could be said in a few abrupt phrases, but the underlying subtext, the emotional state of the character speaking and the context of the speech would be totally lacking. We have too little time these days to afford the luxury of language and the grace of sophisticated expression. Whereas in classical plays, a young man can entrance his loved one with words for a whole evening, now a quick grunt and a bag of popcorn at the movies have to be the substitute.

It is clear then that acting in classical plays requires us to re-evaluate the language and readjust to the experience of speaking and listening so that we become more comfortable with address that has a highly developed form. We have to develop responses to many unfamiliar words and find their nuances of meaning, so that the language is a living, vital, energetic expression of human feeling, not a dusty literary exercise best left on the shelves of a library. For it is true that this language has purpose. Understanding the form as well as the content of what we are saying releases another essential part of the actor's resources. In order to perceive it as another genuine resource it is essential to see the language as a support to the intention and the emotional state of the character; just as one is drawing on all one's intellectual powers to argue something, or to express a need, so one is drawing on all one's capability to express it in the most convincing and persuasive way. It is not random poetry. It is not words for the sake of words. It is the gathering of resource and energy to speak the language with intellectual and emotional influence. It seems that in a world increasingly concerned with commerce, with the exchange and bartering of things, we have limited and to some extent inhibited our sense of an aesthetic as far as communication is concerned. One of the few places where words can be an experience that is both important and beautiful is the theatre. The actor therefore has a duty and a responsibility to value those words, to speak them accurately and appealingly on behalf of the playwright.

How often do we describe things as being 'like' something else these days? In fact the very word 'like' has become debased, serving as it often does as punctuation in conversation, giving it the value of 'er'. Yet the word once had a very direct and powerful use in conversation; it introduced comparisons to support an argument. Shakespeare writes:

> Like as the waves make toward the pebbled shore,
> So do our minutes hasten to their end.
>
> (Sonnet 60)

The meaning is 'We all die some time, and our life is brief'. Yet how much more powerful and evocative is Shakespeare's statement, heightened by the use of the word 'like'. It gives the idea grandeur; it makes it easier to understand and sets an emotional tone to the ensuing sonnet that would not be there with a more prosaic, though equally accurate, statement. It allows for the elevation and expansion of thought; it makes mundane problems universal and brings a sense of scale to the issue at hand.

We are no longer taught the rules for oratory or declamation. As a result we can often be overwhelmed or mystified by the length of a speech. The argument can seem convoluted and difficult to follow. Yet when they are viewed as a whole these speeches have a very definite shape. Our tendency is to ignore this accumulating sense and the value of the shape of the speech in favour of identifying individual small sense groups, each having its own impetus and energy as if they were individual fragmented impulses in the speaker. We speak and think horizontal thought, yet in the longer speeches in classical plays there should be a sense of vertical thought. We should follow through from one thought to the next seeing the connection and development of both sense and intensity in the speaker. The feeling should be not that it is a rehearsed aria but that a process is taking place within the character whose thought evolves and develops. The feeling should be that there is a necessity to express the fundamental idea and an emotional pressure to examine it in order to arrive at some statement of position. It is a good idea to note the places in which the thought changes or takes another tack and then work on all the possible linking thoughts that bring about that shift from one point to another.

Look at this speech of Faulkland's in *The Rivals* and develop the thoughts that are running through his head at the points marked with an oblique stroke:

> Now disappointment on her!/ Defend this, Absolute;/ why don't you defend this?/ Country-dances!/ jigs and reels!/ am I to blame now?/ A minuet I could have forgiven/ – but to be monkeyed for a night!/ – to run the gauntlet through Jack,/ there never can be but one man in the world whom a truly modest and delicate woman ought to pair off with in a country dance;/ and/ even then/ the rest of the couples should be her great-uncles and aunts!/

> (II.i)

You will see that even in a speech that is fairly long, much more is thought than is said. There should always be a sense of compression; that even though one has said so much, there is much more which could be said. Speeches in classical plays can easily become aimless or vacuous when the actor loses sight of the point of the speech or scene. Everything is said with a purpose, and to elicit reaction – this is what gives energy to the performance and precludes self-indulgence. There should be a sense of inevitability in what is said, particularly in long, lyrical passages. If the images and sense and purpose of the speech are well absorbed, then the emotional pressure to gain one's objective reaction from the listener should lend a sense of inevitability to the form and content of the expression. The feeling should be that there is no other way to say this.

Imagine how much more could be said by Oedipus at this electrifying moment in Sophocles' *King Oedipus*. He has suspicions that he has married his own mother and has appealed to her to tell the truth. She refuses and leaves Oedipus, who speaks to the chorus. Imagine the welter of his thoughts and feelings, imagine the sense of compression and inevitability that must be present.

> Let all come out.
> However vile! However base it be,
> I must unlock the secret of my birth.
> The woman, with more than woman's pride, is shamed
> By my low origin. I am the child of Fortune,
> The giver of good, and I shall not be shamed.
> *She* is my mother; my sisters are the Seasons;
> My rising and my falling march with theirs.
> Born thus, I ask to be no other man
> Than that I am, and *will know who I am*.

Remember that everything is not calculated oratory; this is not arbitrary prolixity, but a representation of very human and natural behaviour. Look at this speech from Shakespeare's *King John*. Constance has learned of the death of her little boy, Arthur, whom she believes to be the rightful heir to the throne of England:

> I am not mad: this hair I tear is mine;
> My name is Constance; I was Geoffrey's wife;
> Young Arthur is my son; and he is lost.
> I am not mad; I would to God I were,
> For then 'tis like I should forget myself.
> O, if I could, what grief should I forget! –

(III.iv.45–50)

See how the thoughts are racing through her head as she moves
from one idea to the other. Later in the scene she settles on the
image of her child:

> Grief fills the room up of my absent child,
> Lies in his bed, walks up and down with me,
> Puts on his pretty looks, repeats his words,
> Remembers me of all his gracious parts,
> Stuffs out his vacant garments with his form;
> Then have I reason to be fond of grief.
> Fare you well. Had you such a loss as I,
> I could give better comfort than you do.
>
> > [*She unbinds her hair*]
>
> I will not keep this form upon my head
> When there is such disorder in my wit.
> O Lord, my boy, my Arthur, my fair son,
> My life, my joy, my food, my all the world,
> My widow-comfort, and my sorrow's cure!
>
> > (93–105)

The intensity of the despair is apparent; the images are simple and
embrace all the sensory intimacy of a mother with her young child.
One can almost feel the presence of the child. This is no intellectual argument but a direct emotional statement. The actress
playing it must experience the absence of the child and be filled
with feelings of isolation, revenge, a need for comfort. Constance
has been abandoned on a vast landscape and can see no friendly
face or relief in sight. She is alone, violated and terrified. This could
not be conveyed in one short, factual speech. In fact, for all that
the speech implies, it should feel as if it barely says enough.

Speech is a gesture, just as pointing at someone or moving
towards them or away from them is. It is possible to caress
someone with words just as it is with one's hands. It is an interesting and useful exercise to exchange gestures for words sometimes. What would you do to or with someone instead of speaking
a particular speech? Might you be punching them? Might you be
sitting with your back to them, deliberately ignoring them? This
idea of translating the spoken word to a physical parallel can often
be revealing and can help in identifying the emotional content
and the verbal relationship between characters in a scene.

Just as it is possible to describe the verbal line in terms of a physical act, it is also possible to examine the thoughts from the point

of view that they travel distances and have direction. There is an important dynamic in all human communication in which we express the closeness or distance of our thoughts. It can be heard in conversation, for example, when people are sure of what they are saying and are emphatic in directing it to those who are listening as opposed to people who are unsure and are still identifying the means to express themselves as they talk about something embarrassing. Identifying where the thoughts are going, the distance they travel and the direction they take is very useful. In many public declamatory situations the speaker is sending the thoughts which he or she is articulating a long way to a broad audience, whereas in a very intimate scene, such as the following one between Hamlet and Horatio, with Marcellus and Barnardo in attendance, the nature of the character's interaction is highly intimate, they are together and they are each focusing on one person:

HORATIO
    As I do live, my honoured lord, 'tis true,
    And we did think it writ down in our duty
    To let you know of it.
HAMLET
    Indeed, indeed, sirs; but this troubles me. –
    Hold you the watch tonight?
ALL   We do, my lord.
HAMLET
    Armed, say you?
ALL   Armed, my lord.
HAMLET   From top to toe?
ALL
    My lord, from head to foot.
HAMLET   Then saw you not his face.
HORATIO
    O yes, my lord, he wore his beaver up.
HAMLET
    What looked he? Frowningly?
HORATIO   A countenance more
    In sorrow than in anger.
HAMLET   Pale or red?
HORATIO
    Nay, very pale.
HAMLET   And fixed his eyes upon you?

HORATIO
 Most constantly.
HAMLET
 I would I had been there.

(I.ii.221–33)

Contrast this sense of distance and direction of thought with the end of *The Importance of Being Earnest*, when the stage is filled and the plot is unravelling. Here people are constantly changing distance and direction of thought as each new revelation is made. Some moments are private reflective thought and others public statements.

To take a more detailed example, look at *Richard II*. Northumberland comes to King Richard, who is being escorted to prison on the orders of Bolingbroke, and says, 'My lord, the mind of Bolingbroke is changed. / You must to Pomfret, not unto the Tower . . .' Richard's response to him begins: 'Northumberland, thou ladder wherewithal, / The mounting Bolingbroke ascends my throne . . .' (V.i.51–2, 55–6). These words of Richard's are full of infinite subtlety, some of which may be discovered by examining the nature and then the distance and direction of the thoughts.

Obviously, the first word. 'Northumberland' is a recognition of the person he is talking to, but it also has an exclamatory, reactive quality. Richard's is an immediate response, instinctive and prob-ably derisive. In terms of distance and direction, it is close, focused on Northumberland; it travels only the distance between Richard and Northumberland and is intended for one person's ears. Then follows a qualifying statement, which contains some reflection, some of the intimate history between the two – 'thou ladder', this image is selected. Richard searches for and selects this image, and so the sense of distance between Northumberland and Richard grows greater and Richard's thought becomes more private.

Then Richard explores the landscape of his imagination and experience, referring to his adversary ('wherewithal the mounting Bolingbroke'), and the close focus on Northumberland is exchanged for a broader focus in Richard's imagination, where he reacts to Bolingbroke, the perpetrator of this outrage against his kingship. The confirmation of his worst suspicions is intense as he returns to 'ascends my throne'. His insecurity is a particular and too obsessive part of him that allows him to see things only subjectively, and he always personalises predicaments to learn of yet another grievance. The idea of his throne and the image he has of himself sitting on it is a vital and ever-present image. It is a gilded dream in which he sees majesty not only as an attitude of mind, but also a glorious picture. The distance and the direction of Richard's thoughts change very quickly in these two lines, and this reveals how disturbed he is. The thoughts he articulates are all based on the surprise of Northumberland's statement. Change has been forced upon him, and this shock naturally affects his thinking. His reaction to the messenger and his outrage at the message cause him to lose direction for a moment so that he does not know where to turn or what to say. This is not calculated speaking; it is instinctive reaction.

In drawing attention to this kind of detail I wish to emphasise an important and often ignored element in speaking the text: to whom are you speaking? This question requires the most serious consideration. It is too easy to assume that everything that is said is said in public. This is where the exercise of paraphrasing speeches with another actor can occasionally be helpful. Because we view much of the dialogue in the classical repertoire as being formal speech, we tend to view the whole situation as a formal, very public one, yet if we paraphrase into more informal, collo-quial modern speech, we find that a scene is really a very private, intimate and simple exchange. This is not to deny the existence of very formal declamatory moments in these plays, such as the public statements of the characters in a Greek play or the deliberate formality that Lady Bracknell imposes on most of her interviews; it is simply to say that vocally and intellectually we must be aware of the context and of the fact that there is a great deal of difference between reactive dialogue and calculated, sometimes planned, oratory.

I have always found it useful to take a very quiet rehearsal, where the actors do not feel the need to 'perform' or to consider questions of audibility before they have found the direct sense of the piece. It is also a very useful exercise for the actor working alone. Even learning the words can best be done quietly, not by declaiming the lines so that the music of one's own voice becomes more thrilling than the quiet discovery of the sense. Then when work on the scene begins, the sense of whom one is speaking to should be ever-present. If the person is standing next to you, you should not sound as if you were addressing a crowd in the Roman Colosseum. Remember to speak your lines; don't announce them. Try speaking some of the speeches after you have examined the nearness and remoteness of the thought and carefully defined the person to whom you are speaking. Ask yourself whether a speech is going specifically in the direction of the hearer or away from them. Do you intend them to hear? Or is it entirely for yourself? Where is the thought drawn from, and where is it going? This kind of consideration can help in specifying the character's intentions and provides a focus and incisiveness to the thought, in which the total circumstances of the scene are taken into consideration.

Look at this scene from Act II of *She Stoops to Conquer* between Miss Hardcastle, Miss Neville, Marlow and Hastings. Note where the thoughts are directed and to what distance they seem to travel. Poor Marlow can barely reach Kate Hardcastle with his thoughts, Hastings is coaching Marlow directly and privately, while Kate is extremely direct and invitational with Marlow:

HASTINGS [*introducing them*]

> Miss Hardcastle. Mr Marlow. I'm proud of bringing two persons of such merit together, that only want to know, to esteem each other.

MISS HARDCASTLE [*aside*]

> Now, for meeting my modest gentleman with a demure face, and quite in his own manner. [*After a pause in which he appears very uneasy and disconcerted*] I'm glad of your safe arrival, sir – I'm told you had some accidents by the way.

MARLOW

> Only a few, madam – Yes, we had some. Yes, madam, a good many accidents, but should be sorry – madam – or rather glad of any accidents – that are so agreeably concluded. Hem!

HASTINGS [*to him*]

> You never spoke better in your whole life. Keep it up, and I'll insure you the victory.

MISS HARDCASTLE

> I'm afraid you flatter sir. You that have seen so much of the finest company can find little entertainment in an obscure corner of the country.

MARLOW [*gathering courage*]

I have lived, indeed, in the world, madam; but I have kept very little company. I have been but an observer upon life, madam, while others were enjoying it.

MISS NEVILLE

But that, I am told, is the way to enjoy it at last.

HASTINGS [to him]

Cicero never spoke better. Once more and you are confirmed in assurance forever.

MARLOW [to him]

Hem! Stand by me, then, and when I'm down, throw in a word or two to set me up again.

MISS HARDCASTLE

An observer, like you, upon life, were, I fear, disagreeably employed, since you must have had much more to censure than to approve.

MARLOW

Pardon me, madam. I was always willing to be amused. The folly of most people is rather an object of mirth than uneasiness.

HASTINGS [to him]

Bravo, bravo. Never spoke so well in your whole life. Well, Miss Hardcastle, I see that you and Mr Marlow are going to be very good company. I believe our being here will but embarrass the interview.

MARLOW

Not in the least, Mr Hastings. We like your company of all things. [To him] Zounds! George, sure you won't go? How can you leave us?

The scene continues with many examples of Marlow's attempting to define the distance, direction and therefore the content of his thought. His embarrassment in front of the lady causes him to lunge between formal and informal, between public and private declamation. Meanwhile Miss Hardcastle is entirely focused, her directness, humour and simplicity are all apparent in the way she directs every thought straight to Marlow.

Listening is no less demanding than speaking. If you are able to listen on stage and truly hear the other actor as a character in the play rather than as someone who will give you your cue, you will make your character come to life and will know how to react. This requires practice and focus. Remember that everything that is said in your presence or hearing affects you in some way. Even the guard standing at the door, third from the right, is affected in some way by what is said. I do not mean that every spear carrier is intended to produce a series of grimaces to show that he is listening. Rather his careful listening and the progression of reactions which it produces within the actor keep him as a presence within the scene, not merely someone hired cheaply to don a costume and dress the stage.

The qualities of listening can vary with the anticipated significance of the response and the subject and context in which it is said. It is a useful exercise to study the other actor's dialogue to determine what you hear from him or her which promotes the next speech or piece of action from you. Where do your thoughts change as a result of what you hear? In this respect there are a number of ways to listen:

1. What do you *expect* to hear?
2. What do you *want* to hear?
3. What do you *actually* hear?

Try working through your text, making determinations in respect of these three possibilities. The difference between what you expect to hear and what you actually hear represents surprise for your character. That promotes new thoughts in you. What are those thoughts, and how do you react? There are characters who hear only what they want to hear. Lady Bracknell is one such. Even the proposal scene between Gwendolen and John Worthing in *The Importance of Being Earnest* Act I represents an interesting exercise in listening. One of the dangers of not listening carefully on stage is a very obvious one that all actors fall into from time to time – anticipation. At one level, because of rehearsal, we are well aware of what the other character is going to say; on the other hand the ability to focus only in the moment as it unfolds on stage is a vital one. Otherwise, a mechanical response to the other actor will surely reduce the apparent spontaneity of the action. Never leap in with a predetermined response or behaviour until you have actually heard the words that promote it. Listening each time you give the performance can keep the work fresh and produce a nuance in each presentation which saves it from becoming mechanical.

Listening stirs the energy which keeps the scene and the story moving forward. Listening is about discovery, while speaking is about revelation. There are many surprises in both.

SUMMARY

1. The words support the form and intention of the play.

2. Understand the words, identify them as thoughts and find the emotional impetus to speak them.

3. Listen carefully on stage and use your silence to remain active in thought.

4. Let your reactions be charged by the words spoken to you by another character.

EXERCISES

1. Think of a noun and add the phrase 'is like', then add an image which describes the noun. For example 'The moon is like a huge round cheese'. Then be a little more ambitious and daring in your comparisons. This makes an excellent group exercise in which someone names a subject and everyone else adds an image. The object of the exercise is not only to invent the image, but also to speak the phrase complementing the feeling it expresses.

2. Try speaking in rhyming couplets. It is easier than you think.

3. As a group, have each person bring a new word to the class. Have everyone speak a sentence using the word with the meaning they believe it has. Everyone should at least make a guess. Then the person suggesting the word should reveal the true meaning.

4. In pairs, speak a speech to each other, at the same time. When you have both finished, paraphrase what you heard of the other person's speech.

5. Identify certain short phrases to a partner, then speak your speech. When you come to the phrases you have identified stop speaking and allow your partner to insert them. Begin with a small number of phrases, say two or three, and as you become more practised add more. Note how carefully you listen when you have a function and distinct objective to fulfil.

6. Choose a scene and play it entirely as if all the thoughts expressed are intended to travel a long distance.

7. Redo the scene playing entirely to yourself.

8. Do it again balancing the distance and the direction of the thought. Find those moments when your distance and direction are to the other character, and those moments when the thoughts are to yourself or reach out beyond the other person.

9. Do the scene again varying the way you hear the other character. For example, imagine that everything you hear is a total surprise. Do it as if everything that is said is exactly what you expected. Do it again as if everything that is said is what you wanted to hear.

6
Speaking verse

QUANTITY AND SENSE

I would define verse as relating to matters of structure, like rhythm and rhyme, whereas poetry pertains to the content, the ideas. Thus we may have verse without poetry and poetry which is not necessarily verse. For example, the prose of Thomas Hardy, or many other great novelists, contains poetry but is clearly not structured as verse.

The various structures have been given names which hark back to the classical Greek forms; the most familiar one is probably iambic pentameter. This term has no reference to the poetic quality of the writing but only to the physical arrangement of the verse. Since this is the most commonly used form in classical literature, it is the one to which I shall refer.

Simply stated, iambic pentameter is a term which defines the line length and the rhythm of the piece. How do we know what rhythm is? Listen to your own heartbeat. There are pulses and silences alternating at regular intervals. So it is with language. Rhythm has a definite, regular pulse. That pulse is usually expressed in speech by the degree of loudness with which the syllable is uttered; consequently the rhythm in speech is manifest by the arrangement of loud and soft syllables, the louder ones being referred to as stressed and the quieter ones as unstressed syllables. For example, in the word 'depart' there are two syllables, 'de' and 'part'. We generally speak the first syllable with less force (and therefore more quietly) than 'part', which is spoken more forcefully. 'De' is unstressed and 'part' is stressed.

In a line of verse the author arranges the order of the stressed and unstressed syllables so that they occur regularly. In *Henry V*, the Chorus speaks the following:

> Now 'enter'tain con'jecture 'of a 'time
> When 'creeping 'murmur 'and the 'poring 'dark
> Fills 'the wide 'vessel 'of the 'uni'verse
>
> (IV.Chorus 1–3)

The stressed syllables are indicated by the preceding '. You will notice that they occur on every other syllable, so the rhythm is one unstressed syllable, followed by one stressed syllable, which can be represented graphically as .' The whole pattern for the line would look like this:

$$. \, ' \, . \, ' \, . \, ' \, . \, ' \, . \, '$$

Try speaking the piece placing stress on the syllables preceded by ' and you will hear a pulse similar to a heartbeat. This pattern of unstressed/stressed is given the name iambic. You will notice that in each line there are five repeats of that pattern – hence the name pentameter. So, a line which has five repeats of unstressed/stressed syllables is known as iambic pentameter. Each repeat is known as a 'foot'. Therefore in each of the three lines quoted there are five feet.

The difficulty in attempting to achieve regularity in rhythm in the English language is that the stress is not always placed on the same syllable in every word having a certain number of syllables. For example, in a three-syllable word such as 'fabulous' the stress lies on the first syllable, whereas in 'devoted' and many other three-syllable words the stress occurs on the second syllable. When we see a new word we cannot immediately determine where the stress will lie. English has a free stress system as opposed to many other languages which have fixed stress systems. For instance, in Polish, the stress always falls on the penultimate (next to the last) syllable.

We can determine something of earlier pronunciations of words from this rhythmic expectation. The city of Milan, for example, which we now pronounce with stress on the second syllable, does not fit rhythmically in Shakespeare's plays unless the stress is put on the first syllable. This suggests that the stress has altered since Shakespeare's day.

So we meet an immediate challenge in speaking verse. While the pulse, or let us call it the metre, of the piece may indicate that the syllables follow a pattern of unstressed followed by stressed, the fact is that certain words are not usually spoken that way, or we may be giving stress to a word that is not important to the sense of the piece. When you tried speaking the short passage above, quoted from *Henry V*, while you were able to lilt away with the rhythm, it probably did not make much sense. The final word, 'universe', for example, is not usually spoken with two stresses; we do not customarily place stress on the final syllable, 'verse'. Also, to make complete sense of the piece we would normally not stress the 'of' in the first line. So, if we are to speak these lines with any approximation to the customary form of speech and to reinforce the sense, we obviously have to make some adjustment. What can be done?

Clearly, there is a difference between the stress that we use as a rhythmic pulse and the stress we use to indicate and reinforce sense. The 'di dum di dum' pulse with which you first read this piece can therefore be called metric stress and the variety which emphasises the sense can be called sense stress. If we could bring about a balance between metric stress and sense stress, we would no doubt find a satisfactory answer to the challenge of conveying both structure and sense.

Look back at the definition of rhythm and the line: we observed that it was a pentameter, that is it had five of the recurring patterns of unstressed and stressed syllables. That is the 'quantity' of the line. If we could retain the quantity of the line while demonstrating the sense, we should certainly have gone a long way in retaining the form of the verse. So let us try.

We know we have five stressed syllables in the line. Look where they are and then take the inappropriate ones away and put them in a better position for sense. In effect what we are doing is trading stressed syllables, so that we do not lose the overall quantity of them in a line but reposition them.

> Now 'enter'tain con'jecture 'of a 'time

In reviewing this line, the word 'of' has no importance to the sense and does not need stressing. Think of it as a telegram. If words cost money and I wanted to convey the sense while using the minimum number of words, I would probably send the following:

> Now entertain conjecture time

These are the words which should achieve prominence when we speak them. So we take the stress from 'of', which leaves us with a line with only four stresses. Obviously this does not retain the quantity of the line, which we said was important. However, there is one word in the telegram which does not have a stress whereas we said it should: 'Now'. So having said we might trade stresses, let us give the stress we took from 'of' and give it to 'Now'. That puts five stressed syllables in the line and retains the quantity of the line. It now reads:

'Now 'enter'tain con'jecture of a 'time

Read this aloud, making sure you only put the stress on the syllables that are marked. It should sound much more natural and, if you count the stressed syllables, you will see that there are five, just as there were in the original metrical line. So we have retained the quantity of the line as well as enhancing and endorsing the sense.

Look at the second line:

When 'creeping 'murmur 'and the 'poring 'dark

Again we have examples of words that usually, for sense, would not be stressed. Let us do the telegram exercise again: the words we would send to another person to make sense with the minimum of words are: 'When', 'creeping', 'murmur', 'poring', 'dark'. The word 'and' would not be given stress to enhance the sense. However, we would want to stress the unstressed word 'When'. We can trade again. Take the stress away from 'and' and give it to 'When'. So now the line would read:

'When 'creeping 'murmur and the 'poring 'dark

Again, it sounds more natural while retaining the all-important quantity of the line.

It is vital to remember that all the foregoing is a matter of interpretation. There are no rules about the sense. You determine the sense yourself and then do the re-arrangement if necessary. There are no hard and fast rules that a line has to be spoken one way only, or that there is only one conceivable interpretation of the sense of any given line or speech. There are complexities of character and context that may change what is an immediate, superficial sense. For example, I may say 'I love you', but I could mean 'I hate you'. I could mean I love *you*, specifically, as opposed to someone else. The choices are legion, and they are the province of each individual actor. What has been suggested thus far is offered to help in maintaining the verse structure while supporting the sense which you have determined. There is no point in speaking form without sense, or you will sound like a metronome.

I am not suggesting that anyone acting in a verse play has to go laboriously through the entire text this way. Quite often one's own rhythmic instincts and response to the sense will carry one through, but it is a useful technique when a problem is encountered. Also note that there are many lines in Shakespeare and other classical literature written in verse which do not necessarily conform to the general anticipated rhythmic structure. Sometimes there will be short lines (they do not have five beats) and sometimes there are longer ones. Do not try to force them into five beats; or it will destroy the form and the sense. There are many instances where the change in the form and the quantity of the line has a distinct dramatic purpose, and you should be aware of them. Whenever the form seems to change, this is a signal to take a careful look at the text to see if there is a dramatic reason why this happens. In Act IV of *A Midsummer Night's Dream*, Titania speaks verse, while Bottom speaks prose:

TITANIA
What, wilt thou hear some music, my sweet love?
BOTTOM
I have a reasonable good ear in music. Let's have the tongs and the bones.
TITANIA
Or say, sweet love, what thou desir'st to eat?
BOTTOM
Truly, a peck of provender. I could munch your good dry oats. Methinks I have a great desire to a bottle of hay. Good hay, sweet hay, hath no fellow.

(IV.i.27–33)

The contrast between the mystical and romantic fairy queen and the down-to-earth weaver is well demonstrated by this juxtaposition of prose and verse: it also supports the context. Look also at the changes of rhythm, the varying quantities of a line, in any of the Greek choruses. The short line and the chasing rhythms can denote the urgency and gathering of impending tragedy. From the rhythm we may learn something of the author's intention regarding the pace of a scene.

Referring to *A Midsummer Night's Dream* again, look at the Fairy's speech in Act II, when she meets Puck. She describes herself as wandering 'everywhere, / Swifter than the moon's sphere', and the verse structure supports this description. It also provides a marked contrast to the previous scene, in which we have seen the artisans of Athens making arrangements for the performance of their naive play before the Duke.

FAIRY

> Over hill, over dale,
>> Thorough bush, thorough brier,
> Over park, over pale,
>> Thorough flood, thorough fire:
> I do wander everywhere
> Swifter than the moonës sphere,
> And I serve the Fairy Queen
> To dew her orbs upon the green.
> The cowslips tall her pensioners be,
> In their gold coats spots you see;
> Those be rubies, fairy favours;
> In those freckles live their savours.
> I must go seek some dewdrops here,
> And hang a pearl in every cowslip's ear.

(II.i.2–15)

Do not assume that all Shakespeare's plays are written in verse. *The Comedy of Errors* and *The Merry Wives of Windsor*, for example, are predominantly prose, and any attempt to turn them into verse will be fruitless. Be aware of changes from verse to prose, as in the case of the 'rude mechanicals' in *A Midsummer Night's Dream*. Dramatically there must be a contrast between the speech of these characters and that of the rest of the characters, so that the moment when they speak bad verse in their play of 'Pyramus and Thisbe' is much more telling. If the entire cast has been speaking verse badly throughout the production, the point is lost.

We established that 'quantity' is a term to be used in connection with the length of a line. When we are looking at the line on the page, we can clearly see where the line ends, but speaking it is not nearly so simple. There are many instances where the sense flows onto another line and the natural instinct of any speaker is to continue speaking without any break or any indication that the line ends midway through the sense. On the other hand we cannot just stop at the end of every line to demonstrate quantity. There are other ways of dealing with this. In English it is a natural characteristic of the intonational patterns (the tune with which we speak) to inflect upwards with the voice when we wish to suspend the sense. This can be a very impressive swoop upwards on the last syllable or the merest hint of the note rising. Usually when we are completing sense in everyday speech we inflect downwards. If you are in doubt about what this means, say the word 'No' as a very emphatic statement of refusal. You will hear the voice falling as you say the word. It has a 'downward inflection'. Then say the word as if you were very doubtful about something and want to hear further information. You will hear the voice rising as you say it. It has a 'rising (upward) inflection'.

It is common in English to end a sentence or phrase with a rising inflection where the sense is incomplete, or where a reply is invited. Notice that when you begin a sentence and are interrupted, your voice is rising at the end. Given that this is the common indication that the sense is incomplete, we can apply this principle to the speaking of verse, so that those lines which are incomplete in sense have a rising inflection. This is the way in which we can mark the length of line, establishing its quantity metrically while at the same time suspending the sense so that the listener expects the speaker to continue because the sense is incomplete.

Look once again at the three lines from *Henry V*

> Now entertain conjecture of a time
> When creeping murmur and the poring dark
> Fills the wide vessel of the universe.

You will see that the sense continues through the three lines and is not completed until the end of the third line. Try speaking this on one breath, not stopping at the ends of lines. You will hear that it sounds like prose. Then try speaking the lines with an upward inflection on the words 'time' and 'dark' and a downward inflection on the final syllable of 'universe'. You can allow time at the end of each line to take a breath if you need or wish to before proceeding to the next line. Here you should observe that the sense is suspended and seems to continue, but the length of the line is marked. Not only does this serve to continue the sense and demonstrate the quantity of the line, but it also gives the speaking a certain energy, a feeling of movement forward. It attracts and sustains the interest of the listener. Try it again speaking with downward inflections at the ends of all three lines, and you will perceive how boring the sound is. It makes every line sound as if it is complete in itself and the listener soon loses interest.

The value of the upward inflection is not exclusive to the speaking of verse. It is an absolute necessity in all acting. If you look at the extended, intricate prose of the eighteenth century, or some of the long speeches that Bernard Shaw writes in his final acts, the audience's interest cannot be sustained without upward inflections. Even modern colloquial drama, with short, halting lines between actors, needs the upward inflection.

SUMMARY

1. Balance metric stress with sense stress.

2. Retain the quantity of a line.

3. Note the changes in rhythm and examine their dramatic use.

4. Use the upward inflection for continuing sense.

EXERCISES

When to the sessions of sweet silent thought
I summon up remembrance of things past,
I sigh the lack of many a thing I sought,
And with old woes new wail my dear time's waste.
Then can I drown an eye unused to flow,
For precious friends hid in death's dateless night,
And weep afresh love's long-since-cancelled woe,
And moan th'expense of many a vanished sight.
Then can I grieve at grievances foregone,
And heavily from woe to woe tell o'er
The sad account of fore-bemoanèd moan,
Which I new pay as if not paid before.
     But if the while I think on thee, dear friend,
     All losses are restored and sorrows end.
                 WILLIAM SHAKESPEARE

1. Using the sonnet (or any one of your choice) mark the metric stress and read it emphasising that stress.

2. Review where the metric stress occurs and see if the sonnet makes sense.

3. Adjust the stresses in any line to endorse the sense and retain the quantity.

4. Note where the sense continues onto another line, as in 'And heavily from woe to woe tell o'er / The sad account of forebemoaned moan'. Try reading this with an upward inflection on 'o'er' to suspend the sense and mark the line ending.

5. Choose an extended speech from any classical play or a prologue from one of the eighteenth-century plays and apply the process above. Remember this is not only a technical exercise, just to mark in stressed and unstressed beats. The exercise is to find the form of the verse and see how it supports and endorses the sense. At all stages of determining the sense stress you should relate your decisions to what you mean when you speak the words.

7

Public or private

WHAT YOU KNOW AND WHERE YOU ARE

Public and private behaviour in plays presents a very important and realistic dynamic which gives plausibility to the performance. In chapter 5, referring to distance and direction of thought, I alluded to the idea that one should examine carefully where one's thoughts are going, whether they are intended to be heard directly, overheard or not heard at all. Our behaviour also changes in relation to the context in which the behaviour takes place. So we should consider this from two major points of view.

The first consideration is the personal disposition of the character – the thoughts that he or she is prepared to disclose (the public thoughts) and those which he or she is not willing to disclose (private thoughts). A good example of this is Iago in *Othello*. His public persona as devoted friend to Othello is very different from the private Iago who plots the downfall of the noble Moor. In public he keeps many secrets; in private, when he soliloquizes before the audience, we learn of private matters that are directly contrary to his public behaviour. In working on the text it is useful to go through it determining what your character knows that others do not. Do you make determined efforts to hide this, or indeed is the point of the play that those secrets which you keep privately are gradually or suddenly revealed? Discovery is one of the constantly recurring themes in classical literature and is an integral part of the structure of many of the plays. Disguise is frequently an important part of the plot. The moment in *As You Like It*, Act V, scene iv, when Rosalind reveals herself to be Rosalind and not a boy is a powerful and climactic moment. The secrets (or private lives) of characters are very often the prime motivators for most of their actions and need to be defined in detail. Sometimes they are calculated, as in the case of Rosalind; sometimes they are almost unknown to the characters themselves.

Hamlet goes through much of the play not disclosing his private feelings in public. We learn of them because we are privy not just to the public occasions, but also to the private ones in which he clearly discloses what he thinks and feels. In fact it might be said that part of the tragedy in the play is related to Hamlet's inability to reveal his private thoughts publicly and that further he cannot distinguish between private and public behaviour. So he carries his private grief into a public arena, and while he does not disclose his true private feelings they prompt him to inappropriate public behaviour. In the play scene, Hamlet uses a highly public situation, to work out a private grievance with Claudius and his mother, Gertrude. We know the extent of Hamlet's grief because we saw that most luminous of scenes earlier on in which he meets the Ghost of his father. Here is one of the most breathtaking, excruciating scenes ever written in which a father and son tell each other of things that are so deep, loving, mystical, intimate that it can be almost unbearable to watch. This revelation of private feelings provides an audience with the opportunity to see what drives the rest of Hamlet's erratic public behaviour; it shows us what he is concealing, and we realise that the compression must be great.

It is helpful to review the role you are playing from the point of view of when something new is revealed. It is often a deliberate act on the part of the character, and the reasons for doing so should be noted. This is usually part of the whole scheme for the character's development and can provide a basis for showing growth in the playing of it. The consideration of private thoughts of characters often relates directly to the questions 'Who is telling the truth? and when?' When someone is telling a lie, is it done deliberately? In our earlier example, we would say that Iago is deliberately practising deception and that he is a very accomplished liar. On the other hand there are other circumstances in which the character may not be telling what we know to be the truth but is doing so through ignorance, not because they are accomplished liars, like Iago. Many of the plays of the eighteenth and nineteenth centuries depend on some kind of deception being practised, and it is worth looking at whether this is an erratic, spontaneous necessity to overcome some situation that has arisen by surprise or a deliberate strategy to achieve a pre-determined objective. When Kate Hardcastle in *She Stoops to Conquer* pretends that she is a maid and that her father's house is an inn, she develops a convincing strategy, and her ability to play the lie is a foundation for much of the ensuing comedy. On the other hand in *The Importance of Being Earnest*, the bumbling mistakes of John Worthing, while attempting to live the lie of Algernon's death also provide much comedy. Whether a character tells the lie well or badly is important to many of the plots. Frequently in classical plays the absolute truth is revealed in private moments and the deceptions are played out in public.

The second important consideration in a character's behaviour is the circumstances in which the scene is played. For example, in *Julius Caesar* the Marc Antony who kneels by the body of the newly assassinated Caesar in the capital is very different in behaviour from the Marc Antony who speaks to the crowd shortly afterwards. His behaviour is influenced by the fact that one scene is private and the other public. I have seen many scenes set in drawing rooms that gave the impression that all the characters believed they were on a football field. Most classical plays give clear indications of where a scene is taking place, and these should not be ignored. The tone and quality of the scenes played in the drawing rooms of Bernard Shaw's plays, for example, should be very different from the scene at the beginning of *Pygmalion* where there is a crowd of people sheltering from the pouring rain in Covent Garden.

A perfect example of where the place, the time of day and the overall circumstances affect the playing of a scene is in Act II of *Macbeth*. Macbeth returns from murdering Duncan and is met by Lady Macbeth, who has been waiting for him, fearful that he has not achieved the dreadful objective. She fears 'The attempt and not the deed confounds us'. Macbeth enters:

MACBETH
I have done the deed. Did'st thou not hear a noise?
LADY MACBETH
I heard the owl scream and the crickets cry.
Did not you speak?
MACBETH   When?
LADY MACBETH   Now.
MACBETH   As I descended?
LADY MACBETH
Ay.
MACBETH   Hark! – Who lies i'th' second chamber?
LADY MACBETH
Donalbain.
MACBETH   [*looking at his hands*] This is a sorry sight.
(II.ii.14–18)

57

In this scene it is vital to convey that this is the dead of night (Shakespeare has already established this fact), they are in an echoing, granite castle, lit by burning tapers that cast awesome shadows and every sound will resonate around the corridors. Macbeth approaches the door of Duncan's chamber and enters, passes the sleeping grooms and goes into the King's bedroom. He takes not just one dagger but at least two ('Why did you bring the daggers from the place, they must lie there?'), and plunges them into the flesh of a man. The sensations of the dagger driving through skin and flesh and grinding against bone, then being withdrawn, bloody and warm, are vivid and must play their part in Macbeth's state of mind. He leaves and goes back downstairs. In the silence, every sound is significant to this traumatised man; he carries the daggers, the blood is on his hands and the horror is yet to come. We see in the fractured sentences quoted above – revealed in the structure of the verse – the terror and the silence. 'Did you not hear a noise?', whispers Macbeth. This is not a complete line. His wife replies. Then the realisation and the horror begins. Macbeth has blood on his hands and is unable to control himself. The circumstances dictate secrecy, and Macbeth may not be able to exercise self-restraint. Lady Macbeth is desperate to quieten him and prevent possible exposure. She is extremely aware of the time and the place and the potential danger. He has brought the daggers from the chamber where they should have been left as part of the evidence against the sleeping grooms. This scene cannot be played convincingly, with any conviction or persuasion, unless the circumstances which lie imbedded in the words are fulfilled. The economy and simplicity of what is said belies a highly complicated situation, and the actor must embody those details of time and place. And what happens to a man's body when every fibre, every nerve has been aroused? He will sleep no more. We later hear what sleep means to him: 'Sleep that knits up the ravelled sleave of care / The death of each day's life, sore labour's bath, / Balm of hurt minds . . .' (35–7) The longing for rest, here so finely written, has to be shown, so that the sense of loss is truly appreciated. They are conspirators and murderers, not only of a man, but of a king. This scene is probably as private as any in literature. The actors must take note of the circumstances because the dramatic quality of the scene will be destroyed if it is played loudly or publicly.

Besides considering the location in which a scene takes place, it is also necessary to look at other circumstances which might influence the playing of it, such as the time of day or even the weather. Sometimes there is a very good reason for a scene taking place at night. In *As You Like It*, Act II, scene iii when Orlando returns from the court he meets old Adam in the dead of night. Adam tells Orlando of his brother's plot to kill him. This very sensitive and secret scene depends for much of its tension on the fact that the two characters are meeting furtively; it also says much of Adam that in spite of his age he has waited up for Orlando to return. From this very circumstance and the nature of the meeting, we learn of Adam's nobleness of character and his profound affection for and loyalty to Orlando. It also shows the lengths to which the elder brother has gone to have his way and the evil that this must represent if someone so amiable and honest as Adam is disaffected.

Remember you cannot actually play where you are, nor can you play the time of day as objectives of your performance – the objectives are related to what you want to achieve, but the circumstances in which that takes place are important to the manner in which the objective is pursued.

SUMMARY

1. Note the private thoughts versus the public revelations of the character.

2. At what point are private thoughts revealed? What is the reason for doing so?

3. Is your character telling the truth or telling lies? Is this deliberate or through ignorance? Is your character accomplished at it? Is it part of a strategy, or is it in response to a circumstance to save the character from embarrassment or humiliation?

4. What are the circumstances in which the scene takes place? Is it a big public occasion or a small, intimate interaction? What time of day is it? Where are you? Who is with you?

5. You can only act the objectives of a scene, not the circumstances, but you can allow the circumstances to influence how you behave in pursuit of your objectives.

EXERCISES

1. Working on a scene or speech, change the context from public to private or vice versa. For example, take the scene quoted above between Macbeth and Lady Macbeth and do it as if it were a very public dialogue.

2. Change the circumstances. The scene should be played as if it were bright daylight and in the open air. Use this contrast to return to the scene and discover its intimacy. There are many ways to do this: for example, if you choose a scene where a quiet tea is being served, change the place and try the scene as if it were in a fast food cafeteria.

3. Working in a group, have each member of the group tell a personal story, either a true one or a complete fabrication. The other members of the group should guess whether it is true or false, after they have been allowed to ask questions to determine its authenticity. Note the amount of focus, concentration and detail you have to summon to support the story.

4. Working on a role, note for yourself where your character is telling the absolute truth and where telling a lie.

8

Voice and speech

EXPRESSING FEELING, CLARIFYING MEANING

Much has been written already on this important subject, since the voice is the primary instrument of the actor and an inability to control the voice or to articulate the words distinctly is a significant impediment to any performance. It is not my intention here to provide an exhaustive method of training for the voice and speech, but rather to emphasise some of the essentials which should be explored in greater depth elsewhere.

To begin with we should distinguish between 'voice' and 'speech'. Voice is the sound produced; it is the means by which one may know who is speaking but not necessarily know what they are saying. Voice is common to everyone; speech is personal, regional, national. Speech is the pattern which we imprint on the voice. Once the basic sound has been uttered, the specific shapes we give it are the elements which make up speech.

In producing voice and speech there is an important sequence which, when recognised, allows for a reasonable analysis of the whole process. All utterance begins with the breath, which excites the vocal cords. These vibrate producing a note which passes into the hollow cavities of the throat and face; there the note is amplified, producing a tone, and the tone is shaped by the use of the lips and tongue into units which become words. Each part of the sequence deserves consideration and warrants exercise, since it can influence the whole. For example, inadequate use of the breath can influence the quality of the tone produced, the power of the voice, the definition of the words. Knowing what each part can contribute and what the potential weaknesses may be can enhance one's ability to analyse and work on the appropriate part of the vocal sequence.

Breathing

The breath is the foundation for all good voice production. The objective should be to take easy breaths that can be controlled in force and duration as they are released.

Breathing essentially controls two things: power, which manifests itself as the degree of loudness of a voice, and duration, the length of continuous supported vocalisation. These are alternatives. One cannot use the voice at both maximum power and maximum duration. The actor who wants to speak the whole of the 'St Crispin's Day' speech yelling at the top of his voice is doomed to disappointment, as well as a very red face and the possible loss of his instrument. So it is important to find the appropriate phrasing for any given speech. If you are going to speak something very loudly, then the phrases will be a good deal shorter than if you do it quietly. All exercise for the breath should be calculated to increase the force with which the breath is expelled, to enhance the capability of volume and the control to sustain the duration of the time it takes to expel the breath. At all times one should be careful not to over-extend oneself. The development of good breath control may take a long time and should be pursued progressively, moving on to another stage only once the previous one has been achieved. The simple mnemonic 'Comfort, capacity and control' should be borne in mind. Everything should be comfortable, with no sense of stress; the objective is to increase capacity and control.

Note and tone

It is impossible to consider note independently of tone since once the note has been made by the vibrating vocal cords it must pass into the hollow cavities of the throat and face, where it acquires tone, in order to be heard. It is this aspect of voice production which can be one of the most vexing and demanding to change. We have a number of notes which we can effectively use with our voice, and the objective is to acquire as many as possible that are produced easily and agilely. The ability to use a wide range of notes (or at least have them at one's disposal) is a very important attribute in an actor's performance. There is nothing more soporific than a monotonous voice. The actor who in some highly emotional scene hits the absolute top of his range and then stays there piping becomes impotent. Instead of showing the power and authority which informs his role he does completely the reverse. He shows that he has reached his extreme and has no reserves of either physical force or emotional power. This is extremely dangerous in the classical repertoire. Where speeches tend to be long, with extended emotional intensity, it is vital that every note in the actor's voice is available to reflect subtlety. In talking of 'range' in a voice, we are usually referring to the number of notes which can be produced.

Tone refers to the quality of a voice and is directly related to the placement of it. For example, some people have what we may describe as 'nasal' voices, meaning that they put either too much of their voice through the nose, or not enough – the 'cold-in-the-nose' kind of sound. In many books on the actor's voice and speech you will see reference to 'resonance' and it is this resonance in the varying hollow cavities which defines the tone of the voice. Principally, we have hollow cavities or resonators in the throat above the Adam's apple, in the mouth and in the nose. The object in producing balanced, listenable tone is to achieve appropriate resonance in each of those cavities, so that one is not emphasised above the other. Too much resonance in the throat, for example, can produce a very muddy, plummy sort of voice, which might be suitable for someone playing Marley's Ghost in *A Christmas Carol* but in general is not very attractive or useful. Without the support of a good breathing habit, much of the quality in the voice can be lost and the notes one is capable of producing may be limited. To test this, breathe out and then try to produce the highest note you can. Even if you reach it, it will sound thin at best. So, as the note refers to the range in the voice, tone refers to the quality of the sound.

Any regime for the improvement of the voice should include exercises that:

1. allow all possible notes in the actor's voice to be produced at
2. every possible degree of loudness, with
3. all the varying resonances.

The word

The word is the pattern imprinted upon the basic sound or voice. The clarity with which the words are spoken is the most important factor in making them comprehensible. When an actor is told 'I can't hear', the instinct is frequently to create more voice, that is, to say the words more loudly. But the problem is usually not one of volume but of indistinct shaping of the words. It is possible to be heard on most stages even if one is whispering, provided the articulation of the words is very well defined. The lips and the tongue play a very important part in this, since the agility and strength with which they make the movements necessary to shape the various sounds is directly related to the character of the sound itself. Words are made up of two kinds of sounds: consonants and vowels.

Consonants form the boundaries of words and syllables and usually have some kind of interrupted passage through the mouth. For example 'p' is formed by closing the lips while air builds up behind them; the lips then part, allowing the air to escape in an unvoiced explosion. 'F' is formed by bringing the teeth and the lips close together so that the air is forced between them with audible friction. Consonants carry the major responsibility for the sense of a word. Indeed without them it is impossible to know what a person is saying. Think, for example, of the words that are distinguished by one solitary consonant sound: words like 'made', 'mate', 'male', 'mane'. We have to hear the consonants 'd', 't', 'l' and 'n' in order to differentiate between the words. On the other hand, it has been said that it is possible to change every vowel sound in a speech to one single sound and still be understood provided the consonants are clear and well defined. (Try it with 'To be, or not to be', changing every vowel sound to the 'u' sound as in 'the', but retaining the clarity and distinction of the consonants.) Consonants can also be effective in contributing to the poetry and emotional sense of a piece. When Juliet says, 'I have a faint cold fear thrills through my veins, / That almost freezes up the heat of life,' (IV, iii) the consonants contribute to the feeling of coldness which she is experiencing. These lines also illustrate the dexterity with which one must move from sound to sound, as you will see if you try saying them very quickly. Since it is the lips and tongue that have to make the movements for these sounds, it is important to exercise them for strength and agility; they should be able to move accurately and quickly to the positions for all the consonant sounds.

If the consonants can be described as carrying the sense of a word, the vowels carry the emotions. They are the sounds that reveal the colour or quality of the voice which allows us to understand the emotional state of the speaker. Technically, the vowels are those sounds which have an uninterrupted passage through the mouth. There is no friction or complete stoppage, and they can be continued for whatever duration we determine. They have individual character and are formed by the changing positions of the tongue and the lips. The importance of the vowels in carrying the poetry cannot be over-estimated. The effective balance between meaning and feeling must always be retained, remembering that no matter how lyrical a piece may be, the music of the words is meaningless and self-indulgent without the sense. Look at this scene between Lorenzo and Jessica from *The Merchant of Venice*. While it represents a balmy, moonlit night, in which these two lovers declare their feelings, and the power of their vows is amplified by the poetic expression, the music and vocal line must not override the specific tender feelings which they express:

LORENZO
    The moon shines bright. In such a night as this,
    When the sweet wind did gently kiss the trees
    And they did make no noise – in such a night
    Troilus, methinks, mounted the Trojan walls,
    And sighed his soul toward the Grecian tents
    Where Cressid lay that night.
JESSICA   In such a night
    Did Thisbe fearfully o'ertrip the dew
    And saw the lion's shadow ere himself,
    And ran dismayed away.
LORENZO   In such a night
    Stood Dido with a willow in her hand
    Upon the wild sea banks, and waft her love
    To come again to Carthage.
JESSICA   In such a night
    Medea gatherèd the enchanted herbs
    That did renew old Aeson.
LORENZO   In such a night
    Did Jessica steal from the wealthy Jew,
    And with an unthrift love did run from Venice
    As far as Belmont.

JESSICA   In such a night
  Did young Lorenzo swear he loved her well,
  Stealing her soul and many vows of faith,
  And ne'er a true one.
LORENZO   In such a night
  Did pretty Jessica, like a little shrew,
  Slander her lover, and he forgave it her.
JESSICA
  I would outnight you, did nobody come.
  But hark, I hear the footing of a man.

(V.i.1–24)

The overall objective in developing the voice and speech necessary to perform classical roles is to produce a responsive instrument fully capable of expressing feeling while imparting meaning. The danger in consciously working to improve the instrument often leads to self-consciousness. Remember that the technical work needed to develop the voice and enhance the speech is only the preparation. It is not necessary to demonstrate proficiency in everything, every time one speaks, nor is technical skill ever a substitute for the ability to act. A violinist who is lucky enough to own a Stradivarius does not walk on to a concert platform and wave it around in the air for all to see. He tucks it discreetly under his chin and plays great music. In the same way the actor deploys vocal and articulatory accomplishment as a resource, and technical decisions are made in response to a consideration of the character and the circumstances, not the other way round.

The maintenance of a healthy responsive instrument is a major responsibility for an actor; good vocal hygiene and the avoidance of mismanagement or abuse are imperatives. Regular daily vocal exercise is just as important to the actor as training is to an athlete. After all, the actor is a vocal athlete, and the demands placed on a voice in a major classical role are equal to the demands put on a runner's body. In this regard, watch out for the surest sign of vocal mismanagement, hoarseness. As soon as the voice begins to go raspy, it is an indication that the voice is probably overtaxed in some way. Check that everything you are doing is supported by breath and that you are not over-extending yourself in long, loud passages. If the hoarseness continues to develop, rest the voice. In this case rest does not mean whispering; it means absolute silence until the voice recovers.

SUMMARY

1. Voice and speech are the actor's principal assets and equally one of the greatest dangers.

2. Consonants carry sense; vowels carry emotion.

3. The voice should be capable of agile, confident movement in pitch, volume and placement.

4. Breathing is the basis of all good voice and speech.

5. Breathing accounts for power or duration of speaking.

6. Do not display the instrument; play the music.

7. Find the balance between poetic expression and meaning.

8. Practise daily, so that technique can be a support not a concern.

EXERCISES

The following exercises are provided as a basic warm-up for the voice and speech. They cover each aspect referred to in this chapter but are not intended to be the means by which you can train the instrument. There are many good books on the subject, though these do not replace work done with a good teacher.

1. Breathe in gently to a count of three and breathe out to a count of five. Make sure you maintain the breath at equal pressure on the outgoing breath line.

2. Increase the count for the expiration of the breath to ten, to fifteen, to twenty. Make sure that you remain comfortable with each stage. Beware of raising the shoulders as you breathe in. Try to remain relaxed.

3. After repeating the above exercises several times whisper the count, making sure there is no rasp in the throat.

4. Do the above exercises again, but this time speak the words quietly.

5. Hum any tune gently, feeling the vibrations in the mask of the face. It sometimes help to lick the lips, so that you can feel them tickling as you do this.

6. Intone 'Moo Moo Moo. Mah Mah Mah. Mee Mee Mee.' Check that the sound which you hear on 'ee' is as full and rich as on 'oo'. Do this fairly rapidly, ensuring that you hear a continuous humming sound through the entire sequence.

7. Count up to ten as if you are asking a series of questions (with an upward inflection).

8. Count up to ten as if you are making a series of very dogmatic statements (with a downward inflection).

9. Repeat exercises 7 and 8 alternating the upward and downward inflections, so that odd numbers have an upward inflection and even numbers a downward inflection.

10. Repeat 'lalalala lalalala lalalala' several times.

11. Repeat 'will you won't you' several times. Make sure it does not become 'will you won'tchew'. Exaggerate the lip movements.

12. Read any piece of prose very fast, exaggerating the movements of the lips and tongue and with exaggerated changes of pitch and volume. Repeat this several times.

9

Doings, gestures and demeanours

MOVEMENT AND GOOD MANNERS

Most classical plays that represent something of the everyday life of the people were written in a time when appearance and good manners were considered as important as the inner emotional and intellectual life of a person. Indeed, the outward appearance and physical condition of a person were considered a true reflection of who that person was. Even Plato, writing in *The Republic* says 'Simplicity in life produces bodily health, just as it produces temperance in the soul.' This suggests that a cultivated man should be able to direct his life physically and ethically so that he would not need to see a doctor or end up in the courts. Plato asserts that physical education, no less than education in literature and the arts, really has to do with the soul. The two together should provide a harmony in the human personality. This idea was related not only to matters of behaviour, but also to dress and the way that a person recognised and deferred to others.

Most classical plays deal with a stratified society in which certain people were considered superior to others and there was a distinction between men, women and children. All had their 'place' and each deserved a certain kind of behaviour from the other. There were rules of behaviour appropriate to each group. In this stratified society the ultimate deference was to God, then to the king and down through the various ranks of courtier to the common man. Men had superiority over women, and children were supposed to be little adults with no right to assert themselves. The Victorian maxim 'Children should be seen and not heard' was a precept that was held in earlier ages as well. There may have been distinctions and exceptions within individual families; what took place privately may in fact have been quite distinct from what was expected in public.

It should be remembered that these outward signs of inward grace were inculcated from the earliest years and were not self-conscious demonstrations; the actor who wishes to reflect the physical life of a character in earlier times has the difficult task of making the behaviour seem familiar and comfortable. In the stratified societies of which we speak references to people of 'good breeding' are legion. One's position on the social ladder depended largely on birth. Wealth and privilege were usually inherited, although in every age there were those who rose in rank through the acquisition of money or through exceptional deeds or marriage. The higher up the ladder one was, the more authority one had. This was an expectation. There was no need to assert or constantly claim authority in such a society, because it was an inherent right. Lady Bracknell, for example, assumes authority; she had an inherent expectation from birth that she would be obeyed by those beneath her on the social ladder. There is no need for her to shout or struggle for dominance; she asserts her right as a lady, not as a Billingsgate fishwife. Similarly, when playing royalty, there is no need to play 'being king'; the behaviour of others will reflect that authority.

There are many examples of comedy predicated on the aspirations of middle-class people who wish to be regarded as upper class. *The Clandestine Marriage* by Garrick and Coleman is one superb example, in which Mr Sterling, who has made money in that terrible thing called 'commerce', apes all the outward appearance of the gentry. Of course everything is done to excess. In his play *London Times* Sir Arthur Pinero shows the middle class desperately and comically trying to be accepted into society in London.

The lower and middle classes were not the only ones who were treated to satire and ridicule. There are also members of society who are the objects of comedy. Sir Fopling Flutter in *The Man of Mode* by Sir George Etherege is one of those who imitates the fashions of the French and becomes a parody of the exaggeration that the more restrained English saw in the clothes and manners of their European counterparts.

While we cannot wholly assume all the intricate niceties of manners and deportment that were prevalent in any age, it is important to understand some of the principles behind such courtesies and what they were intended to achieve. In trying to simplify this matter from the point of view of the stage, it seems to me that they fall into four major categories:

1. Greeting
2. Leaving
3. Conduct in the presence of others
4. Characteristic business for the time, place or character.

In a magazine from the middle of the nineteenth century we read a fair encapsulation of the objectives of such etiquette; the author claims that he writes 'Showing the means by which people are gracefully and easily introduced to one another. Pleasant acquaintance made, resulting often in lasting friendship.'

The following are some specific recommendations, taken from various authorities, which may be useful in obtaining a sense of what is required. Like clothes, the fashions in manners change (indeed some of the changes were directly related to what it was possible to do in the current clothing fashion) and so, for convenience I have taken very general periods, where major change has taken place. They are not exhaustive lists of all the changes, but are intended to give some indication of what might be appropriate in each of the periods.

The Middle Ages

Greeting and leaving

When greeting or leaving a superior, a man was expected to bow. This bow is taken directly from a genuflection in church in which one 'bows' one's knees to God. Generally, a man would only kneel on both knees as a sign of honour and adoration of his God; in front of men he would kneel on one knee. Kneeling, even if on one knee, was regarded as a very formal bow. More frequently the man would place one foot behind him, the feet parallel, not turned out, incline the body forward slightly and bend both knees. The weight would be distributed equally between both feet. The effect would be rather as if one intended to kneel but arrested it half-way. During the bow the headwear would be removed, be it a hat or the cowl on a cloak. A hat would be held at the side of the thigh, with the inside of the hat concealed from the person to whom respect was being shown, no doubt to avoid revealing its greasy condition.

71

The woman's curtsy had many similarities to the man's bow, although while we have noted that men would kneel on both knees only to God, women might go on both knees to men of much higher station. Again, this full curtsy was reserved for highly formal situations, and in more everyday greeting the woman would half-kneel, like the man. Sometimes she might keep her feet together and bend the knees in an informal curtsy, sometimes known as a 'bob', which could be seen even in Victorian times.

Bows and curtsies were used on meeting and leaving others and on entering and leaving a room in which someone of superior or equal rank was present. Children were bred to be miniatures of their parents and so boys and girls would learn very early to bow and curtsy at the same times and places as their parents.

Conduct in the presence of others

One major principle, which persisted right through to the nineteenth century, was that an inferior should not speak until spoken to, and that one should remain quiet and attentive, ready to be of service. Nothing harsh, loud or crude in one's behaviour should be allowed to intrude on the orderly conduct of conversation and business. There should be nothing that drew attention to a person of lower station in the presence of superiors. In fact the more one was able to be present without exciting the awareness of that presence the better.

The Elizabethan era

Greeting and leaving

While the bow and the curtsy remained the most formal and respectful form of greeting or leaving someone, between gentlemen doffing or clasping hands was also acceptable. In the practice of these formalities there were often excesses. In many of the plays of this period, continuing through the seventeenth and eighteenth centuries, we see characters who have taken the basic formalities and exaggerated them to comic excess. Many of the fashions in England were derived from the other European courts, and the attempts of some people to associate themselves with a kind of sophistication and superiority as a result of travel and knowledge led them to adopt such fashions, vainly aping their superiors, only to bring ridicule on themselves.

The bow for the man was a continuation of the idea of bending one's knee. A courtier was taught to move the left foot behind the right, as he stepped backwards and to bend the knee of the left leg, while keeping the right one straight in front of him. The hat would be removed at the same time and taken to the side of the body. The weight would now be firmly over the left foot, and the torso open and exposed to the person being greeted. In curtsying women either continued to move one foot behind them and genuflect, or kept the feet together and bent both knees in the more informal 'bob'.

Doffing the hat exposed the head, which is the noblest part of man, and thus did honour to whoever received this greeting. The hat was removed by the brim and held to the side of the body, again avoiding exposing the inside, and then the other hand was kissed towards the person being greeted. This doffing of the hat could be done alone or as the introduction to a bow. The removal of the hat, a kiss of the hand and a step backwards with a bending of the back knee would complete the very formal bow. In this period hats were not removed when stepping indoors, or at meals. When greeting some one it was expected that the gloves would be removed.

Conduct in the presence of others

Men and women were advised not to sit too far back in a chair, so that both feet could be firmly placed on the ground and, in the case of the women, so that the farthingale did not cause the dress to shoot up at the front. Sitting with legs apart, or sprawling back in the chair was distinctly frowned on.

In moving around a room men were particularly cautioned about their rapiers, and when sitting they were expected to have the weapon placed point forward, along the line of the leg. The man would appear more graceful if he rested one arm along the arm of the chair and rested the other on the elbow. He might hold something in his hand such as a glove or a handkerchief. In most of these respects the lady was expected to do the same, though she might also fan herself gently; otherwise the hands could be held demurely in the lap.

Characteristic business

This is the period in which the fan was introduced. This was not the folding fan of later periods but rather something resembling a table tennis bat, though much lighter. It is this kind of fan that the Nurse demands of Peter in *Romeo and Juliet*. They could be highly decorated with painting or embroidery and the stick would be attached to a long cord or chain, allowing the bearer to drop the fan, which hung from the waist. Both men and women used fans. It should be remembered in handling the fan that it was not only a means of cooling, but could be used for discreet communication with others. The temptation to waft the fan continually should be resisted.

With the introduction of tobacco, pipe smoking and snuff-taking became very popular, although not everyone approved of the habit. King James I himself wrote a famous treatise entitled *Counterblast to Tobacco* in which he railed on the indiscretion of smokers who filled the room with acrid smoke and blew their smoke across the table during meals.

Both gentlemen and ladies carried pomanders, small metal spheres that were intricately designed and worked, sometimes with separate segments like that of an orange, in which various perfumes were carried. No doubt they were needed to ward off the smells of a society whose concept of sanitation was very remote from ours. For example, chamber pots were frequently emptied from upstairs rooms into the street.

It is in this period that handkerchiefs were introduced, and highly delicate and intricately decorated examples would be carried by both men and women.

The seventeenth century

Greeting and leaving

It was in the seventeenth century that the bending of the knees in a bow or curtsy became less important and the forward inclination of the body came into fashion. The leg was moved forward instead of to the back at the beginning of the bow, the body was inclined forward and this action might also be accompanied by the kissing of one's own hand and the drawing of a figure of eight in the air with the hand and arm which removed the hat. While men now bent the body, women continued to bend their knees. The two forms of greeting, grow increasingly dissimilar from this time on. Like the bow the curtsy would take a number of forms. In both cases there were versions for entering and leaving and other versions for greeting and for passing people. For a very formal curtsy the lady now lifted her heels, with her feet together, made a slight inclination of the body and bent her knees. She lowered her eyes as she lowered her body, returning to look at the person to whom she was curtsying as she rose. Both men and women would modify the depth and extent of the bow or curtsy according to the time and place and the importance of the person to whom they were showing deference.

The kissing of hands was prevalent in this period as a gesture of respect to someone else and also when receiving an object. This could be a cumbersome activity because one was expected to remove one's gloves before doing so. It has little application in a play because of the awkwardness and the amount of time it takes.

Conduct in the presence of others

The rules of conversation and intrusive behaviour in front of superiors continued to obtain. Meanwhile, the obligations and duty of a gentleman towards a lady increased. A gentleman was expected to offer a lady verbal compliments, take her hand as an escort when walking, assist her to be seated and open doors for her entry into a room.

Up to this period dropping food from the table to the floor and spitting were not frowned upon, but as people of quality acquired fine carpets and furnishings spitting became taboo.

Walking was taken very seriously, and particularly towards the end of this century the dancing master who taught deportment would spend much time in teaching the correct way to walk. Anyone taking long strides was considered ill bred. Men now began to turn their feet outward from the hip and were expected to walk at a modest pace, never hurrying or bobbing up and down. Women were expected to walk with their feet close together and turned slightly outwards.

Characteristic business

Pipe smoking continued, as did the taking of snuff. The means by which one did those things became increasingly refined and intricate. Snuff was often carried in small, highly decorated boxes, sometimes with a very small spoon from which the snuff would be inhaled. It was considered good manners to offer the snuff to another, though an inferior would not take that initiative in front of some one superior to him.

The eighteenth century

The eighteenth century shows many signs of a society we would recognise, in which those brought up in an earlier time were puzzled and sometimes appalled at the changes brought about by the young. Instead of a studied formal attitude to manners, this century was one of elegance and a kind of discreet but calculated negligence.

Greeting and leaving

In this period the bow showed the effects of the dancing master's training. The person bowing removed his hat from his head directly to his side (though in this case the inside of the hat was shown to the person receiving the bow, no doubt because with the wearing of wigs there was no longer a need to conceal the grease inside), one leg was placed forward, with the knee straight and the toe pointed and touching the ground; the back leg was turned out and bent. Then the body was bent from the waist, while the man bowing first looked at the person to whom he was bowing and then lowered his eyes as he bent over, regaining eye contact as he rose from the bow. The lady's curtsy was similar to this bow, except that after taking the weight on the back foot and bending the knee she recovered forward with the weight transferred to the front leg which was also bent at the knee. Sometimes the shoulder nearest to the person being greeted was turned away as the curtsy was made.

Conduct in the presence of others

The costumes of the period, with their heavy corsetting and boning both in women's and frequently in men's clothes, allowed for very little movement of the spine and so posture became very upright. Constant activity with handkerchiefs fans or snuff was frowned upon. An easy, relaxed deportment in company with no distracting or superfluous movement was expected.

In walking the man was expected to take moderate steps placing the heel first and keeping the body erect, with the feet slightly turned out. The woman was required to walk with short smooth steps and to give the appearance of gliding. Her body was held erect and her hands held in front of her at waist level with the palms turned upward and inward.

It is just in the eighteenth century that children were allowed to walk alongside their parents rather than behind them. The costumes of the period did not allow the woman to recline in any way and she had to sit on the edge of her chair, with a straight back and her hands laid elegantly in her lap. Men continued to wear their hats indoors and were cautioned against loud and vulgar laughter. It was considered very ill manners to burst into guffaws or make loud reactions to anything.

Characteristic business

Tobacco continued in use, and there are many accounts of women both smoking and taking snuff; many rules were written as to how snuff might courteously be taken.

One of the great features of this period was the fan. By now it was the folding variety with which we are familiar. In themselves they were wonderful works of art, lacquered, painted, decorated with lace or made from wood or bone. Ladies used them not only for cooling themselves but to good effect as a means of expression in company. Since it is one of the favourite properties of any one playing in an eighteenth century play, the following language of the fan is provided to give some ideas for its use.

Holding the fan

1. Hold the closed fan with the thumb and forefinger of the right hand and place the body of the fan in the left hand, or

2. Hold the fan closed with the tip in the palm of the right hand and the bottom of the fan in the palm of the left hand. One hand should be directly above the other.

Language

Touching the lips with a closed fan means 'shhh, be quiet', touching the right cheek means 'Yes' and the left cheek 'No'. Touching the nose means 'I don't trust you' and touching the forehead means, as might be expected, 'You're crazy'.

Hiding the eyes with an open fan means 'I love you' and holding the fan above the head means 'I can't have anything to do with you'. Quick brushing movements with the open fan mean 'I don't love you' and slowly lowering the fan and pointing it to the ground means 'I despise you'.

The nineteenth century

In some respects the nineteenth century is easier to deal with. Although some behaviour may still seem strange, deportment in general becomes a good deal easier.

Greeting and leaving

It was in the nineteenth century that the bow and the curtsy gave way to the handshake as the most popular form of greeting. Here is one set of advice which was offered in *Hill's Manual of Social and Business Forms* by Professor Thomas E. Hill:

> Accompanying the salutation of hand-shaking, it is common, according to the customs of English-speaking people, to inquire concerning the health, news etc.
>
> Offer the whole hand. It is an insult and indicates snobbery, to present two fingers when shaking hands. It is also insulting to return a warm, cordial greeting with a lifeless hand and evident indifference of manner, when hand-shaking. Present a cordial grasp and clasp the hand firmly, shaking it warmly for a period of two of three seconds, and then relinquishing the grasp entirely. It is rude to grasp the hand very tightly or to shake it over-vigorously. To hold it a very long time is often very embarrassing, and is a breach of etiquette. It is always the lady's privilege to extend the hand first. In her own house a lady should give her hand to every guest.

If both parties wear gloves, it is not necessary that each remove them in shaking hands; if one, however, has ungloved hands, it is courtesy for the other to remove the glove, unless in so doing it would cause an awkward pause; in which case apologize for not removing it, by saying, 'Excuse my glove'. The words and forms will always very much depend upon circumstances, of which individuals can themselves best judge. Kid and other thin gloves are not expected to be removed in hand-shaking; hence, apology is only necessary for the non-removal of the thick, heavy glove.

As a rule in all salutations, it is well not to exhibit too much haste. The cool, deliberate person is the most likely to avoid mistakes. The nervous, quick-motioned, impulsive individual will need to make deliberate a matter of study; else, when acting on the spur of the moment, with possibly slight embarrassment, ludicrous errors are liable to be made. In shaking hands, as an evidence of cordiality, regard and respect, offer the right hand, unless the same be engaged; in which case, apologize, by saying, 'Excuse my left hand'. It is the right hand that carries the sword in time of war, and its extension is emblematic of friendliness in time of peace.

Conduct in the presence of others

The rules concerning the assistance of ladies still applied. When a lady walked into a room, the expectation was that the men would stand until she was seated. Similarly if a lady left the room, the gentlemen stood until she had done so.

The following taken from *Hill's Manual of Social and Business Forms* by Professor Thomas E. Hill will provide a thorough indication of what was expected:

What should be avoided when calling

Do not stare around the room.

Do not take a dog or small child.

Do not linger at the dinner hour.

Do not lay aside the bonnet at a formal call.

Do not fidget with your cane, hat or parasol.

Do not make a call of ceremony on a wet day.

Do not turn your back to one seated near you.

Do not touch the piano, unless invited to do so.

Do not handle ornaments or furniture in the room.

Do not make a display of consulting your watch.

Do not go to the room of an invalid, unless invited.

Do not remove the gloves when making a formal call.

Do not continue the call longer when conversation begins to lag.

Do not remain when you find the lady on the point of going out.

Do not make the first call if you are a new-comer in the neighbourhood.

Do not open or shut doors or windows or alter the arrangement of the room.

Do not enter a room without first knocking and receiving an invitation to come in.

Do not resume your seat after having risen to go, unless for important reasons.

Do not introduce politics, religion or weighty topics for conversation when making calls.

Do not tattle. Do not speak ill of your neighbours. Do not carry gossip from one family to another.

Characteristic business

Smoking continued and had become very well established, though there were firmer rules about where and when one might do so. No man would smoke in the company of a lady, for example. (One should note this when doing *The Importance of Being Earnest*; if Jack and Algernon have been smoking before the arrival of Lady Bracknell, they should destroy the evidence.) At dinner parties it was customary at the end of the meal for the ladies to retire for conversation, while the men remained, possibly to smoke and drink port.

Parasols were often used by ladies, although that favourite stage device, the fan, became less evident. It became smaller and was reserved for special occasions like a visit to the opera. For men, visiting cards, cigarette cases and pocket watches all found their place in the nineteenth century, together with handkerchiefs, gloves, umbrellas and walking sticks.

This summary of behaviours appropriate in various periods should not be taken as exhaustive. There are many other curious facts to be found, with the appropriate research. This should not only be encouraged; the actor should see it as a definite obligation. Much can be contributed to an individual performance as well as to the concept of an entire production by careful research. For example, research into the history of medicine would be very valuable when one is doing a production of Molière's *Imaginary Invalid*. The kinds of implements used and the understanding of the social position of doctors at the time is all-important to the tone and accuracy of the presentation.

Of course the physicality of the actor is not exclusively dependent on the information we may have about a certain period. There are many important decisions to be made about what will best express the individuality and personality of the character we are playing. Sometimes there are very clear statements about characteristics from the playwright (for example the hunch back and the limp of Richard III) or they can be implied. Tony Lumpkin in *She Stoops to Conquer* cannot have the same physical bearing as Marlow or Hastings. Tony is a country boy, born and bred; he finds the bowing and scraping of the town people pointless and unnecessary. He does not wear the same clothes and has a recklessness of attitude, with no sense of deference either to his mother or to strangers. This gauche and ill-bred attitude must be reflected not only in his speech and what he is saying, but also in his general deportment. He is physically inept and clumsy. How does Anne Boleyn in *Henry VIII* bear herself in front of a whole court of men, as a wife pleading to the king, her husband, for her life? She addresses him, 'Sir, I desire you do me right' (II.iv.11). Her use of 'Sir' instead of his name is a very important clue. She is portrayed as a woman of great inner strength and dignity. She has humility and is fully aware of the seriousness of her situation. I think she is probably kneeling, which serves to intensify the situation and reinforce the distance between her husband and herself. She is being cast off, reduced to the level of everyone else who comes before this awesome body to appeal. The sadness, the nobility, the humility that this simple gesture implies is very affecting and that one word, 'Sir', is a springboard into the rest of her plangent and eloquent protestation of fidelity and love.

Contrast this with Paulina in *The Winter's Tale*. She has a sense of self-possession and her own worth and dignity. I think she does not kneel when she makes a similar plea. Rather she stands, head erect, not cowed by her autocratic husband. She speaks candidly and simply to her husband, seeking his understanding and faith in her.

At first these appear to be two very similar situations, but the personalities are different and, therefore, their physical appearance must reflect that. There are different rhythms, different tempos and different feelings of the physical strength of each. These differences are the stuff on which one can act. It is a very useful exercise to define very honestly how one sees oneself physically and then draw the contrasts between that profile and the character one is playing. In most cases the rhythm will be different, and the strength and tempo of the actor will be altered in response to the examination of the character and his or her situation.

Look for those rhythms and have words to describe them, because it is useful to write them in a script as one is preparing a role. They can be written at the beginning of each scene as a reminder to put aside habitual movement and characteristics in order to assume the physical life of the other character. For example, if you are lively and staccato in rhythm and physical response, it can be very difficult to rid yourself of these characteristics to play a character who is slower and has more weight than you do. Even a simple, 'Slow, heavy' written at the head of the scene can be a help in reminding you of the change you must make to play the character. Beware of personal habits, also, that intrude on your ability to assume the body of another person. They can be simple things, like stroking your hair, or a particular walk. In doing a profile of yourself it is important to be thorough and severe. Ideally every actor should have a neutral gear, as it were, with no defining physical characteristic, from which to begin to assume the life of a character. This is ideal, but it is also equally useful to know what you might do, what are the habits that you apply to almost every role, almost as a defence mechanism when you are uncertain or ill prepared. There is much to be discovered in the physical preparation of a role; sometimes the simplest of things go unnoticed and yet they need consideration. This is Laurence Olivier's account of finding the walk for Othello in his book *On Acting*:

A walk . . . I needed a walk. I must relax my feet. Get the right balance, not too taut, not too loose. Walk with poise. It wasn't working. I couldn't make it work. The movement, the rhythm that I needed wasn't there. I watched. I studied – nothing. I should walk like a soft black leopard. Sensuous. He should grow from the earth, the rich brown earth, warmed by the sun. I took off my shoes and then my socks. Barefoot, I felt the movement come to me. Slowly it came: lithe, dignified and sensual. Lilting, yet positive.

Olivier's ability to metamorphose or transform physically was remarkable. But he also put himself through rigorous exercise and maintained a fitness that allowed his body to respond to all the creative ideas and impulses that his talent generated. Fitness cannot be too heavily emphasised. There is no doubt that plays in the classical repertoire are emotionally and intellectually demanding on an actor, but they are also physically demanding. The body is as important a part of the actor's instrument as the voice. Just as regular and consistent work is required to tune the voice and hone the diction, so a well-conditioned and well-tuned physical instrument is necessary. Not only are you preparing yourself against the physical exhaustion that can be attendant on playing a major classical role, you are also ensuring that there is never a time when you have an idea but are physically incapable of carrying it out.

SUMMARY

1. Research and understand the physical expectations of the period.

2. Be aware of the physical clues that a text yields. They may be direct or be implied within the script.

3. Create a physical profile of yourself against which you can contrast the physical appearance of your character.

4. Beware of habitual physical defences that prevent you from becoming the character.

5. Stay fit and have your body tuned and as responsive to impulses as the voice.

EXERCISES

1. Try all the bows or curtsys described in this chapter.

2. Take movement classes and stay fit.

3. Create a detailed physical profile of yourself, including all your physical habits. Use it to create character profiles of roles you are playing or wish to play. How would you have to change? Look at the tempo, rhythm, weight and kind of flow you give to movements like walking and sitting.

4. Observe someone you see on a regular basis and note in detail their mannerisms and physical characteristics. Write a complete physical profile of them. It is very useful to develop the facility of analysing movement and physical behaviour. You can build a vocabulary of movement in this way just as you can acquire words.

10
Nothing that can be explained

IMAGINATION AND DARING

So far our concern in this book has been with research into the background of the play and its context, which should help in developing characters and understanding the events which form the play. The knowledge that has been gained about the style, form and context of the play is only so much intellectual information unless the actor uses it in acting. Many classical plays have a universality of theme, but it is important to beware that this does not lead to a general type of acting in which archetypes and clichés abound. You cannot play a king, a fop or an *ingénue*, except in a general way, and the portrayal will have no dimension or development unless you specify which king, fop or *ingénue*. There is a huge difference between the personalities and actions of King Creon and King Richard III, of Sir Benjamin Backbite and Sir Fopling Flutter and of Lydia Languish and Cecily Cardew.

To express this another way, we must beware of playing characteristics rather than characters. Sometimes those characteristics are so strong and seductive that they are almost overwhelming; for example, Richard III describes his physical deformities very clearly, and it is a great temptation to let that represent the character, rather than using it as information to delve into the personality of Richard and specify the dimensions of his behaviour scene to scene, moment to moment. The aim should be to bring the force of a three-dimensional character to the stage rather than reinforce the distance of time and language by generalising. In this regard there is a danger of playing the theme of a play rather than the specific moments of an individual's circumstances. To take the case of Richard III again, he is not just an evil, hunch-backed villain who ascends the throne. He is a complicated, plausible politician; he has humour; he can be wry and ironic. The way he deals with rejection, his need for recognition and status, his pursuit of personal affirmation all inform his behaviour. The actor playing Richard should beware of playing just one characteristic – evil;

after all, it is not Richard's intent to be hated but to be loved.

The idea of Richard wishing to be loved whilst appearing evil is the encapsulation of an important principle which is worth examining. Often what is manifest in a character to observers is not the private intent of the character. To take another example, Argan in Molière's *Imaginary Invalid* does not wish to be ill. He believes he is ill, but his intent is to be well. Any playing 'in' to the sickness will lead to self-indulgence and two-dimensionality. The humour comes from the extraordinary lengths he will go to in order to be healed. We can see the excessiveness of his actions; he feels only the need to cure himself of all of the maladies which beset him.

Quite often we see in classical literature that the sense characters have of themselves is in direct opposition to what appears to an audience. Obviously, in discussing playing characteristics rather than the character, it is important to acknowledge that every human being does have personal characteristics that are appropriate, personal and often inescapable. They are the things that, in a cursory description, people may use to define an individual, but they are not ultimately the things which provide intimate knowledge of that person; they bring about recognition but not necessarily understanding. Characteristics may be physical – 'She's the tall one with red hair', 'He's the one who says "er" all the time' – or they may be behavioural – 'He's incredibly naive', 'She's such a pessimist'. And while they may aid recognition, they in no way define the intricacy of that person, or take into account the fluctuations of human interaction. You cannot base a character on physical characteristics: you cannot act red hair; you cannot inform an audience wholly about a character only by interpolating 'er' into every sentence. On the other hand the behavioural characteristics may lead in some small part to the understanding of the character since they show typical behaviour. However, that understanding of a character will always be incomplete, bearing in mind that a person does not behave typically all the time, and in fact much drama depends upon the occurrence of atypical events. Typically, Macbeth is a noble, courageous, loyal servant to King Duncan, but in the play we see the tragedy that ensues when he behaves atypically. Othello reveals his love for Desdemona at the beginning of the play, and the tragedy unfolds as he is gradually subverted by Iago. What we have been led to believe is the typical disposition of Othello is corrupted, and Othello behaves uncharacteristically to the extent of murdering Desdemona. Eliza Doolittle in Bernard Shaw's *Pygmalion* may be superficially described as a chirpy cockney flower-girl, brash, good-humoured and affectionate. However, that is not the complete picture; we also see a girl with a fine temper, a sense of her own personal worth and pride, intellectual ability, physical stamina and courage well beyond our initial expectations or a cursory description of her characteristics.

I believe that in studying a role it is most useful to begin by asking: 'What is the typical behaviour of this character?' Once this is answered, look at what events take place in which the character behaves atypically. Remember that it is not always big things that change – good does not always become outright evil, shyness does not always become boldness – but the subtle as well as the blatant shifts of expected behaviour often provide the third dimension to a role, which alleviates the tendency towards generality and cliché. They also provide surprises. This is a most important element of good acting and, therefore, good theatre. There is nothing more boring than predicting exactly what an actor will do and seeing the expectation fulfilled. Even though we may know the story, the revelation of the personalities, not the recognition of them as archetypes, is the major part of any given theatre experience. Many people know *Hamlet* as a story and have seen a number of productions of that play, but the individual actors and directors in any particular interpretation may provide quite new answers to the questions that the play poses. If we play only the naive symbolic characteristics of a role, and if the whole play is conceived on that basis, there will be little sense of interpretation, nothing fresh, nothing challenging and, above all, nothing personal in the performance. I am not suggesting that one has to come up with spurious or manufactured answers to the challenges of an individual play in order to create an 'original' interpretation; fidelity to the intention of the author and the scrupulous search for what one believes to be the essence of the play are always the presiding principles.

One of the most important truths that are demonstrated in the classical repertoire is that *extraordinary circumstances produce extraordinary behaviour*. We know this to be true, for we have all read stories of perfectly ordinary people placed in critical situations who find the courage to perform a heroic act. There are few events that are written about in the body of dramatic literature that are commonplace; generally the story has engaged the playwright's interest because it contains exceptional properties. Although the theme and the concomitant moral may be applicable to many situations, these particular stories are elevated examples of more mundane experiences. This requires the actor to be daring and bold in his or her choices, which presupposes that lack of information or the denial of instincts will only inhibit the real search for the character. In his biography of Sir Donald Wolfit, Ronald Harwood describes just such a moment of extraordinary daring on the part of the actor in playing Lear, the imaginative leap and the detail contained in every moment which elevates the action beyond the commonplace:

> But Lear is more than a father spurned by ungrateful and ambitious children, more than a man whose reason is endangered. 'I gave you all,' he cries, and the actor speaks the line as though aware for the first time of the enormity of his own self-betrayal: it is the King, stripped bare of power and authority. His strength is drained in the argument concerning the number of his retinue, and again he is no more than man, aged, helpless. He turns his back on the audience, crouching low, sobbing into his hands. Regan asks, 'What need one?' Now cries the wind: 'O reason not the need' it pleads, and the actor's voice is burdened with piercing, whining overtones, then is entrapped in despair, '. . . let not women's weapons, water-drops, Stain my man's cheeks!' The vocal thunder cracks. 'No, you unnatural hags' is accompanied by an electrifying effect: Lear's cloak, a wide full circle, swirls in a petrified arc as the King turns upon his daughters, and the actor embarks on the major climax of Lear's mounting crisis.
>
> > I will have such revenges on you both
> > That all the world – I will do such things –
> > What they are, yet I know not, but they shall be
> > The terrors of the earth. You think I'll weep;
> > No, I'll not weep: I have full cause of weeping.
> > But this heart shall break into a hundred thousand flaws,
> > Or ere I'll weep. O fool, I shall go mad!
>
> The 'terrors of the earth', delivered in the nasal register, harsh and grating, is echoed by a thunderclap which seems to arrest the King's anger, for it is the gentle, pitiful frailty of 'O fool, I shall go mad' that finally takes him out on to the heath.

The critic James Agate, writing enthusiastically about this performance in *The Sunday Times*, said, 'Mr Wolfit did nothing which one could explain.' Apparently this performance and the way the actor played it transcended the commonplace, was full of surprises and reached deeply into the revelation of the ageing, tragic king. It disposed of characteristics in favour of the character, took the perfectly ordinary circumstance of a disaffected father arguing with his daughters and elevated it into the extraordinary.

This brings up the most important question an actor can ask during the preparation of a role – 'What if?' This question challenges the imagination, not necessarily the facts, though the answers should be predicated on the given circumstances. It allows for a 'playfulness' in what the actor is doing, and every opportunity should be taken to explore it, just as we did when we were children. A tree can become a monster, and a six-year-old can become a knight or an astronaut. It is that simplicity and imaginative intensity which can convert a stage to a heath and recorded sound into real thunder that causes a mad old king to scream 'howl, howl, howl'. There is a liberation, sometimes ecstasy, in those moments when the question 'What if?' is posed and the actor dares to execute the most extreme of answers. It allows the actor to make many 'offers' in rehearsal, to explore and make discoveries in his or her preparation and is liable to produce personal answers. The actor who arrives at a rehearsal with many ideas is infinitely more exciting than the one who has carefully prepared a limited and cautious strategy which he or she intends to polish during the production's preparation.

The actor must develop daring and freedom to 'play', to pose a possibility in an impossible situation. The reality is that none of us is King Lear or Lady Bracknell, but an actor is charged with the challenge of suspending disbelief and making an audience accept the impossible, of embodying an experience that is so emotionally charged and intellectually informed that belief or non-belief is not an issue. This requires an ability to surrender to a role and not always to work at things. Some factors in the interpretation of a role are not calculable, and the actor's readiness to accept those moments and follow his or her instinctive reactions is vital. These factors often arise in the interaction between actors – when an actor, for example, looks into the eyes of another and something happens that was not planned but feels right. It feels exhilarating and seems to come from nowhere definable. It is assertive of the feeling in a way that cannot be articulated. It is a moment that is recognised by the actor, though he or she may feel that it is too fragile to be described.

How do we cultivate that imagination? How do we release the inhibitions on the actors instinct? Firstly I believe we must not be too literal. Instead of taking everything at face value the actor asks, 'Yes, but, what if?' Do not always assume that the ultimate performance of the role will be the result of the most obvious early responses to the text. Secondly, we must allow things to happen during rehearsal rather than follow some minutely strategised plan. There is always room for reconsideration. The first choices we make are not necessarily the most satisfactory or profound, and we should be alert to the fact that as rehearsal progresses, new meanings may be discovered. Indeed one hopes that they are, as otherwise it would be a very uncreative process. Thirdly, we must be aware of our own tricks, habits and defences against the unusual or demanding. In the early stages of personal preparation or rehearsal, the actor will probably feel uncertain, and the need for survival will be uppermost. This is the very time to beware of easy solutions and superficial answers and to look upon the role and its development as a challenge, rather than a problem. The probability that things are not as they were first thought to be should charge the imagination, and the research and the answers that one comes up with should raise more questions.

Ultimately, playing a role should be a continuing, growing process, because the likelihood of giving the definitive performance of any role is remote. Each performance should still be an adventure, a quest to find the means to fulfil the expectations of the playwright more wholly within the parameters of the agreement with the director and the rest of the company. I am not suggesting here that fundamental changes should be made or that the actor is at liberty to do whatever he or she pleases. After all, the process of rehearsal is also a process of negotiation in which agreements are reached over the essential elements of an individual performance and the structure of the production as a whole. It is important to honour that agreement. The spirit of what is intended should be constant, but the means by which that is best expressed may change somewhat, and this awareness and enthusiasm in finding the best means keeps the play alive and the performance fresh.

SUMMARY

1. Beware of playing characteristics rather than a character.

2. Look for the unexpected events in the story.

3. Remember that characters do not always behave typically; what are the surprises?

4. Extraordinary circumstances produce extraordinary behaviour.

5. Beware of basing a character on physical characteristics.

6. Constantly ask the question 'What if?' and allow yourself to try some of the answers.

EXERCISES

1. In studying a role, examine the emotional, intellectual and physical characteristics of your character and contrast them with yourself. How would you react? What would you do? Define what the character does, and why.

2. Ask yourself 'What if?' In a group, start an improvised scene on any basis; at some point stop, say 'What if?' and then completely change the characters and the circumstances. These can be as eccentric and unconnected as you like. Continue the scene based on the new idea. Do this several times.

3. Choose a scene and play it with what you believe to be the exact opposite of its true intent. Make the tragedy funny and the comedy tragic.

4. Observe someone who interests you and try to imagine their story. Write a monologue for them. Try this in a group or a class with postcards or photographs. Each person takes a picture and then tries to build a story round the person. Avoid pictures of well-known people and use snapshots of anyone.

5. In a group, bring in a very personal object – a watch, an old teddy bear or anything that clearly has personal importance. Develop a character around this prop. Who used it? What were they like?

11

Now I am alone

LONG SPEECHES AND SOLILOQUIES

As every actor does on being cast, you will no doubt immediately look through the script and experience the delight or despair of seeing how big the part is and whether you have any really long speeches. Those extended moments, particularly soliloquies, when the whole of the theatre is focused on you can be a brilliant chance to show off, or an unmanageable passage of time when everyone seems to be waiting for the end of something that is far too long. It need not be that way – indeed it must not be. Like everything else in playing a classical role, they are just another challenge and should be seen as a golden opportunity to reveal more of the character and enhance the understanding of the play.

The first principle, I believe, in approaching these extended moments is not to detach them from the rest of the play. When you are first reading do not skip through them, just gleaning a general sense but not working out their influence on the overall structure of the play. They must become integrated with and organic to the whole conception of the role and the production, not remain isolated purple passages that are independent of the play. I also believe it is a grave mistake to learn them separately, though I realise that this is very much a personal matter. Some actors do not learn in sequence in any case, and this is acceptable, although I think the preferable method is to begin at the beginning and learn the lines in sequence as the character progresses emotionally and intellectually.

If in a performance the audience senses that you are about to begin a long speech, your efforts are doomed from the start. It becomes a comment from the actor on the structure of the play, or his or her attitude towards it. There are many physical cues which can give away this sense of preparation: an adjustment of position, sudden sonority of the voice, the apparent 'settling' of the actor – where he or she indulges in each separate image in the speech – all contribute towards a sense of detachment from the character and the events taking place. This is a particular danger in Shakespeare, where so many of the soliloquies and long speeches are well known, even to an audience. There is a definite problem in playing Jaques in *As You Like It*, for example, and coming to the moment in Act II, scene vii where he begins 'All the world's a stage . . .' – the Seven Ages of Man Speech! The fact that it is labelled is no help at all. But therein may lie a key to the problem, or the stimulus to meet the challenge. First of all dispose of the label. This is not an independent piece of greeting-card wisdom written by William Shakespeare for calligraphers to practise their art on. It is the timely expression of a character within the play in which he reveals a philosophical viewpoint that tells us much about his personality and the relationship he has with the duke and his followers. Look at this speech for a moment and see what it says about the person saying it. Do not be impressed by the neatness of the idea or the poetic images used to express it. Read it, digest the thoughts and then ask yourself 'What kind of person would say that?'

JAQUES
    All the world's a stage,
    And all the men and women merely players.
    They have their exits and their entrances,
    And one man in his time plays many parts,
    His acts being seven ages. At first the infant,
    Mewling and puking in the nurse's arms.
    Then the whining schoolboy with his satchel
    And shining morning face, creeping like snail
    Unwillingly to school. And then the lover,
    Sighing like furnace, with a woeful ballad
    Made to his mistress' eyebrow. Then, a soldier,
    Full of strange oaths, and bearded like the pard,
    Jealous in honour, sudden, and quick in quarrel,
    Seeking the bubble reputation
    Even in the cannon's mouth. And then the justice,
    In fair round belly with good capon lined,
    With eyes severe and beard of formal cut,
    Full of wise saws and modern instances;
    And so he plays his part. The sixth age shifts
    Into the lean and slippered pantaloon,
    With spectacles on nose and pouch on side,
    His youthful hose, well saved, a world too wide
    For his shrunk shank, and his big, manly voice,

Turning again toward childish treble, pipes
And whistles in his sound. Last scene of all,
That ends this strange, eventful history,
Is second childishness and mere oblivion,
Sans teeth, sans eyes, sans taste, sans everything.

(II.vii. 139–166)

Notice that there is a really dangerous moment in this speech, when it is possible to signal the beginning of the independent aria. It comes when Jaques says, 'His acts being seven ages'. That moment between 'ages.' and 'At first' needs great care. It must be related to the context, as the whole of the speech has to be. Why is he saying this? Is it prompted by the presence of Old Adam? Is he making a very special point to the duke about the futility and ridiculousness of man? Many questions have to be answered, including 'How spontaneous is he?' Is this an eloquence that he finds on the spur of the moment? Or is it something which he has prepared on his perambulations round the forest? Is it considered thought or a discovery which he is making? How ready is he with the examples? Did the idea of a ballad to his mistress's eyebrow just flash into his brain and amuse him? What reaction does he expect? He could be playing to the assembled crowd for the approval of his wit and eloquence. Should they applaud him? Does it sadden them? Is there silence after he finishes as each man turns in upon himself and reflects on the mutability of man? Do not regard it as a long speech but as an extended series of thoughts.

Although you may have entered a scene to say what you say, you probably did not intend to say it exactly as it appears. In many of these long speeches we see the struggle of the speaker to find the means to express the thoughts that make the meaning plain to the listeners. Complete sequential fluency of thought and vocabulary is as much a distinguishing factor of a character as the fractured, hesitant speech of a shy person. There is no doubt, for example, that some of the characters in a Shaw play have the immediate wit of Shaw himself, and this should be used as part of their personality. However, most people are somewhere in between and do have to search for thought and expression, often finding eloquence in moments of high passion. The spontaneity of the thoughts and the impromptu quality of their expression must be retained. The focus you muster to convey the thoughts is part of the condition of the character, which reveals not only the character's attitude to the thoughts but his or her reaction to the immediate situation, including the other characters. Anything that reveals the actor's preparation for the extended thought will militate against its effectiveness both for the audience and for the actor.

Listening to these speeches has much of the same challenge for the other actors on the stage. Each time you hear the speech, it should be fresh, it should be new, it should be a revelation. Concentrate on the meaning, not on how the actor is performing the speech. Do not become lazy enough to stop listening because you know how many more lines there are until the end. At any time during rehearsal, it should be possible to stop the speech and ask the listeners what they are thinking and feeling. There should be no one on the stage who cannot give an immediate answer which is relevant to that moment in the play.

Try speaking this speech from *The Rivals* to someone. Ask them what they heard – not just the general sense, but specifics. Have them read it to you. See if you can really listen to all of it.

JULIA

> My soul is opprest with the sorrow at the nature of your misfortune: had these adverse circumstances arisen from a less fatal cause I should have felt strong comfort in the thought that I could now chase from your bosom every doubt of the warm sincerity of my love. My heart has long known no other guardian – I now entrust my person to your honour – we will fly together. When safe from pursuit, my father's will may be fulfilled – and I receive a legal claim to be the partner of your sorrows, and tenderest comforter. Then on the bosom of your wedded Julia, you may lull your keen regret to slumbering, while virtuous love, with a cherub's hand, shall smooth the brow of upbraiding thought, and pluck the thorn from compunction.

(V, i.)

What does it mean? What does it mean within the circumstances? What are the revelations to the listener?

Actors generally lose the audience in these extended speeches because they have lost themselves. It takes a great deal of concentration to maintain the focus. Loss of focus often occurs when the images related to the specific thoughts are not detailed and clear enough to the actor. Again, I remind you that it is not enough to understand the thoughts; the whole thing must be assimilated as a sensual experience. The whole of your awareness – sight, touch, taste, smell – should be engaged and directed towards reflecting the meaning. Extended speeches can represent some of the most private and most intense of a character's thinking, because they relate to his or her unique personal history and experience.

It is helpful to consider soliloquies as a dialogue with yourself. We often see the character acting as a devil's advocate with himself or herself, as in the most famous soliloquy of all, 'To be or not to be'. The thought developed in a soliloquy usually shows the character in a dilemma, coming to a resolution and expressing at the end the determination to take a certain action. Soliloquies very often represent the deciding moment before action. What action is that? Keep in mind as the speech progresses that you are gradually mounting an argument for resolute activity. There are also soliloquies in which people anxiously awaiting an event reveal their most intense inner fears and desires. Their inner emotional turmoil contrasts with the slow, impersonal passing of time. With this conflict as a catalyst, we learn things we might not have learnt, had there not been that imposed restraint. Look what we learn of Juliet – her desires and phantasies and fears – as she impatiently waits for the nurse to return with news of when Romeo will come to her:

JULIET

> Gallop apace, you fiery-footed steeds,
> Towards Phoebus' lodging. Such a waggoner
> As Phaëton would whip you to the west
> And bring in cloudy night immediately.
> Spread thy close curtain, love-performing night,
> That runaways' eyes may wink, and Romeo
> Leap to these arms untalked of and unseen.
> Lovers can see to do their amorous rites
> By their own beauties; or, if love be blind,
> It best agrees with night. Come, civil night,
> Thou sober-suited matron all in black,
> And learn me how to lose a winning match
> Played for a pair of stainless maidenhoods.
> Hood my unmanned blood, bating in my cheeks,
> With thy black mantle till strange love grown bold
> Think true love acted simple modesty.

Come night, come Romeo; come, thou day in night,
For thou wilt lie upon the wings of night
Whiter than new snow on a raven's back.
Come, gentle night; come, loving, black-browed night,
Give me my Romeo, and when I shall die
Take him and cut him out in little stars,
And he will make the face of heaven so fine
That all the world will be in love with night
And pay no worship to the garish sun.
O, I have bought the mansion of a love
But not possessed it, and though I am sold,
Not yet enjoyed. So tedious is this day
As is the night before some festival
To an impatient child that hath new robes
And may not wear them. O, here comes my Nurse . . .
(III.ii.1–31)

This passage tells us so much of Juliet's hopes, and we can relish the whimsy that creates such unusual and very personal images. The idea of cutting Romeo out in 'little stars' is fresh and amusing and also childlike. We see the agility of her brain and the impetuousness of her nature as she flits from one idea to the other. On the other hand, her deep desire for him is seen in the building repetition of the word 'come'.

This speech is also interesting structurally because it follows a pattern of thought found in many speeches in classical literature:

1. The statement of the subject.

2. The amplification of the arguments with examples.

3. The development from the personal statement to a universal landscape of thought.

4. The return to the simple and immediate: 'here comes my Nurse'.

Beware of listening to yourself in these extended speeches; too often the meaning and the character disappear while the actor is deep in the appreciation of his or her own voice. It is not the musicality of the instrument to which one should respond but the discovery of the sense. It is easy to make long speeches an intellectual pose rather than a period of intense emotional negotiation. They should be prepared slowly, thought by thought, image by image.

Another vexed issue which always comes up in considering these solo speeches is 'Should I look at the audience?' My answer would be 'Yes'. I dislike the sense of disconnection when the actor gets a glazed look in his eye, peers at the middle distance and pretends we are not there. I believe that the audience should be embraced as co-conspirators, the character's other self, or a close friend. That open confession in front of the audience brings them deeper into the action, rather than distancing them as cold, objective observers. The character can share the emotion as well as the reasoning with the audience and use that relationship as part of the obstacle to overcome. The contrast between emotional desires and reasonable wants is a very important one; often in these long speeches we see the character arguing what is reasonable against what is desired. Will the character accept reason? Very often they do not, and that is the subject of tragedy. In Greek plays we understand what is reasonable, but the character chooses the other course. Macbeth knows what is reasonable, but his emotional desires and the arguments which Lady Macbeth mounts against reason are overwhelming. Look for this aspect in every long speech you deal with. It is there.

While on the subject of long speeches I would like to add a final word about audition speeches. Always treat them as part of the whole play, particularly speeches from the well-known classical repertoire. They should be prepared as if you were going to play the entire role and not treated as independent entities because you have not read the whole play. You should always assume that whoever is auditioning you has done so. Do not try to be clever, or original, or gimmicky. The intention in an audition is to find out whether you can act. The more you choose and execute the audition speech in order to reveal your good acting, the better off you will be. In choosing material look for something that you find fresh and exciting, something that you feel you have a justified viewpoint about. Most of the speeches in Shakespeare have already been done many times, so do not spend hours looking for obscure speeches or putting together cuttings of several speeches for the sake of originality. It rarely works. You will be left working on a piece that has little personal connection beyond your persistence in finding it. Even the oldest chestnuts can be brought to life and the auditioner's attention held if your acting is superior, if out of careful, imaginative work you have wrought a personality who really comes alive.

SUMMARY

1. Do not think of 'long speeches'; think of them as 'extended thought'.

2. Beware of speeches that are well enough known to have names.

3. Do not signal the start of an extended thought.

4. Learn to listen.

5. Make the speech a sensual experience.

6. Contrast the emotional desires of the character with his or her reasonable wants.

7. Audition speeches should rely on and be examples of good acting.

EXERCISES

1. This is a good exercise in both speaking and listening. Take a passage out of the telephone book and read it to a partner. Your partner should see how many names and numbers he or she can remember. Take some time to review the names; try to give them a life, a personality, an image, because they have a relationship to you. Give the speech an intention. There is a reason why you are listing these names. Try the exercise again. This is something that can be done fairly regularly. It is surprising how much you can improve your ability to listen.

2. Create your own soliloquy. Improvise a situation where you are waiting for something. The matter is urgent; it could even be a matter of life and death. Put yourself into that situation and speak your thoughts aloud. For example, you are waiting for news of whether a relative of yours is involved in a plane crash. Set a place, a time and the other conditions. What is the conflict? How many reasons can you find for hoping that they might be alive, how many for

fearing that they might be dead? What is your desire versus your reasonable assessment.

3. Take any long speech or soliloquy and use it as an explanatory speech. Emphasise the delivery of the facts versus the images. Reverse this.

4. Rehearse your soliloquy or audition speech with someone else.

12
The Greeks

STORY AND RITUAL

I have chosen to write a separate chapter about the Greeks, because I believe the plays and the demands they make have unique qualities and require a different style of acting. These are not plays about real people doing everyday things and consequently they require a different approach.

By comparison with our modern naturalism, the stories in the Greek plays can seem extremely simple, while, paradoxically, their structure seems incredibly complex. In the tragedies, there is no attempt to create suspense and arouse the audience's curiosity about what is going to happen next. A modern audience may not know the story as their forbears did, but the audiences at the festivals at which these plays were originally performed were very familiar with the legends and myths which formed the narrative of the plays. These were stories handed down from generation to generation, like the oral tradition of many other cultures. With each telling they were no doubt enhanced or exaggerated, and the emphases would change according to the teller. Each playwright would recount the essential incidents in a very personal way but, with a particular viewpoint concerning universal moral issues, would demonstrate a thesis concerning man and his relation to the forces informing his actions.

In the tragedies we see the acceptance of fate and the sense that man is puny before the gods, the belief that fate will take a hand and to a large extent control the destiny of human beings. As E. F. Watling wrote, 'At its roots lie not only the human instincts for narrative and impersonation, but also the instinct for ritualistic expression and interpretation of the power of natural forces, the cycle of life and death, and the nexus of past, present, and future.' Through suffering we can all learn; by the example played out before us we can be provoked to a deeper consideration of our relationship, human being to human being, and then to the greater forces who oversee our world. In this respect, the Greek plays have a solemnity and a religious aspect which we can certainly understand, though we may not accept its view of the composition of the universe, with the hierarchy of Gods and their interaction with humankind. We can appreciate the importance of the issues and the common ground on which we stand in relation to where we came from, what choices we have and where we will be going. In these plays we are constantly faced with the dilemma that there are no absolutes of right or wrong and that every action that we take has a consequence which brings either punishment or reward.

The following scene from Euripides' *Electra* perfectly exemplifies this. Electra has finally come face to face with her mother, Clytemnestra, who killed Electra's father. She has waited a long time to take her revenge. The moment has come.

Electra is in the house, and the deed is taking place as the chorus speaks:

CHORUS
 Now retribution follows sin:
 Through the fated house a new wind blows.
 Long ago my beloved lord and king
 Fell dead by the water of purification;
 And through the rooms, round the stone cornice,
 Rang out his death-cry,
 'O wicked, wretched wife, why will you murder me,
 Returned after ten harvests
 Home to my own country?'

 Now like a returning tide
 Justice arraigns the reckless adultress
 Who, when her husband after many years
 Came home to his heaven-high Cyclopean fortress,
 Grasped the whetted axe,
 With her own hand struck and felled him.
 Pity the victim of her vengeance,
 Whatever raging woes possessed her.
 Like a lioness from the mountains
 Roaming through meadows and orchards,
 She carried out her purpose.
CLYTEMNESTRA (*Within*)
 My children, for the gods' sake, don't kill your mother!
CHORUS
 Do you hear that shriek in the house?
CLYTEMNESTRA
 Help! Oh! Oh!

CHORUS 1

She calls for pity, and I pity her,
Done to death by her own children.

CHORUS 2

Soon or late, Heaven dispenses justice.
Poor, desperate queen, your suffering was bitter;
But your revenge on your husband was unholy.

CHORUS

They are coming, clothed in fresh streams of their mother's
blood –
Trophy of triumph over that beseeching cry.
There is no other house, nor ever was, whose fate
More rends the heart, than the great house of Tantalus.

Orestes and Electra emerge from the palace and then realise their
own guilt. While they thought themselves justified and have
brought years of searching and agonising to this point, they
know they should not have committed murder, and so we are left
to ponder the nature of right and wrong. They may have felt
justified in revenging the death of their father, but Orestes points
to the dilemma:

O Phoebus, in the command of your oracle
Justice was hidden from me;
You have made torment clear.
You have bestowed on me, for my obedience,
A murderer's destiny, far from Hellas.
To what city shall I go?
Will any friend, will any man who fears God,
Dare to look in my face –
A son who has killed his mother?

In this example the events are simple but the issues that are raised
are complex. It also illustrates the role of the chorus, which has a
unique place as an actor within the scene and as an auditor and
commentator on the issues. At times the chorus represents the
audience, the ordinary spectator, raising the issues, mulling over
the possibilities, wondering at the behaviour of the principals. So,
like the audience, at times they stand in the middle of the action,
engaged and involved; at other times they withdraw to an objective distance and lyrically and impartially examine the truths
exposed in the play.

This seems very remote from our contemporary expectations

of a play; there is no attempt at 'naturalism', the characters are not explored as personalities but remain as symbols of the drama, though they are not without emotion. They have grand passions, which embody the force not of one person but of a universal, primal identity in which each one of us may see ourselves as Orestes or Electra. The scale and proportion of the emotions expressed raises us above ordinary realistic experience; our cries of pain and despair are insignificant compared with those of an Electra or an Antigone, a Creon or an Oedipus, because this is not the grief of an individual only; it is the rage, the despair, the suffering of all.

It is in the very scale of these dramas that the greatest pitfall lies. The physical appearance of the characters and the detail of physical characterisation is limited, often formal and frequently only symbolic. Few things in the text are merely implied, and so our expectations of understatement or implicit behaviour have to be set aside. There are no restrained glances from which the actor and the audience can read a thousand unstated thoughts. These characters are 'out there' direct, expressing exactly what they mean and feel in an extremely heightened, poetic language, with a strong verse form underpinning it. The actor must therefore avoid responding to all the outward manifestations of the form while missing the essential deeper emotional truth. Somehow we have to find a means, not just to make loud sounds and grand gestures, but to find the seed which when cultivated will grow and flourish as an extension of true human experience, instead of remaining a superficial exhibition of the actor's technique.

Firstly, one should establish what exactly the text means. That demands the application of some of the suggestions on reading a play offered earlier in this book. Before any attempt is made to represent the scale of the drama, quiet, thorough preparation is essential. There are many references that need researching, many details of the story which are taken for granted within the text which have to be revived and assimilated. In preparing *The Trojan Women* by Euripides, for example, the story of the Trojan war should be reviewed. The issues that are posed by the play should be explored. What are the questions that we intend the audience to ponder after seeing the production? What is the dilemma facing each individual in the story? In this respect, if you are playing a member of the chorus, remember that while they represent a body of people, they are also like an individual in the dramatic action. They preserve that individuality, though on many occasions they speak with one voice.

Look carefully at the structure of the play as an overall experience and then identify the specific details of the line-by-line rendering of this experience. The verse form contributes enormously to identifying emotional state and content. The changing rhythms, the length of line, the accruing of meaning and force throughout long speeches all carry import for the audience and represent a resource for the actor. They not only provide a means by which the drama will be enacted but also provide clues as to the nature of the content. The long, studied lines of Teiresias, the blind prophet in Sophocles' *Antigone*, who pronounces on the fate of Creon, give authority, weight and validation to his statements.

TEIRESIAS
    Then hear this. Ere the chariot of the sun
    Has rounded once or twice his wheeling way,
    You shall have given a son of your own loins
    To death, in payment for death – two debts to pay:
    One for the life that you have sent to death,
    The life you have abominably entombed;
    One for the dead still lying above ground
    Unburied, unhonoured, unblest by the gods below.
    You cannot alter this. It follows of necessity
    From what you have done. Even now the avenging Furies,
    The hunters of Hell that follow and destroy,
    Are lying in wait for you, and will have their prey,
    When the evil you have worked for others falls on you.
    Do I speak this for my gain? The time shall come,
    And soon, when your house shall be filled with the lamentation
    Of men and women; and every neighbouring city
    Will be goaded to fury against you, for upon them
    Too the pollution falls when the dogs and vultures
    Bring the defilement of blood to their hearths and altars.
    I have done. You pricked me, and these shafts of wrath
    Will find their mark in your heart. You cannot escape
    The sting of their sharpness.
    Lead me home, my boy.
    Let us leave him to vent his anger on younger ears,
    Or school his mind and tongue to a milder mood
    Than that which now possesses him.
    Lead on.

This contrasts with the urgency of the chorus on Creon's depar-
ture – short, pulsing lines, betraying the excitement and ecstasy
of the moment just before the arrival of the messenger who
announces the death of Haemon.

CHORUS
    O Thou whose name is many,
    Son of the Thunderer, dear child of his Cadmean bride,
    Whose hand is mighty
    In Italia,
    In the hospitable valley
    Of Eleusis,
    And in Thebes,
    The mother-city of thy worshippers,
    Where sweet Ismenus gently watereth
    The soil whence sprang the harvest of the dragon's teeth;

    Where torches on the crested mountains gleam,
    And by Catalia's stream
    The nymph-train in thy dance rejoices,
    When from the ivy-tangled glens
    Of Nysa and from vine-clad plains
    Thou comest to Thebes where the immortal voices
    Sing thy glad strains.

These changes and contrasts in rhythm are essential not only to
the 'pulse' of the play, but also to the pace at which one speaks.
Find those changes of pace. There is nothing more boring than a
solemn, relentless plod through a chorus, a speech or – worse still
– the whole play. The shifting tempos and rhythms are indicators
of the changing internal energies of the characters. *Never mistake
effort for energy.*

    The issue of effort versus energy is a very important principle
in any acting, but particularly in the classics. I have seen many
performances that substitute undue effort for internal impetus.
The feeling created is that the actor is an aggressor towards the
play and the audience and that he or she is forcing through in
spite of all the obstacles placed in the way by the playwright and
the production, even the other members of the cast. The truth is
that the only real obstacle the actor has is his or her own lack of
understanding and sensual connection with the role. The energy
of a role comes directly from the depth of commitment the actor

has to the role and is a reflection of the character, not of the actor. An audience should never be aware of an actor straining and working.

The words used to express the story also reveal the experience of the character. They have to be assimilated as a physical feeling as well as an intellectual experience. In these Greek plays, indeed in the whole of poetic drama, the words not only tell us what something means; they also convey the full sensual (not sexual) connection that the character has with the experience. The mention of blood, for example, is not a pathological statement about plasma and haemoglobin, etc, but about a warm, life-giving liquid, thick, red, odorous and belonging to someone specific. Do not be deceived by the grandeur of the language; it is there because the feelings are more intense, not more remote.

Having read the play and begun to understand the story, the meaning and the means, it is invaluable to read the play aloud to oneself. There is a great deal of information which communicates itself when the words and rhythms are spoken. Allow yourself to read quietly, without immediately responding to the apparent declamatory and literary values. Feel the changing pulses of the components of the play, feel them like blood pulsing through the body, changing as the emotional states change. In this limited way also feel the restraint imposed by this quiet approach to the text. There are moments when you will wish to cry aloud, but resist it. This is useful later, since part of the preparation should be concerned with the compression that the figures in the tragedy feel. We must never think that they have reached their limit in emotional compass or in what can happen to them. Similarly, the actor in these plays should never have reached the full extent of his or her technique. There should always be just a little more. In Euripides' *Medea*, Jason finally confronts Medea, his wife, who has murdered their children and sits in a chariot above him with the bodies of the two children by her side:

You abomination! Of all women most detested
By every god, by me, by the whole human race!
You could endure – a mother – to lift a sword against
Your own little ones; to leave me childless, my life wrecked,
After such murder do you outface both Sun and Earth –
Guilty of gross pollution? May the gods blast your life!

It would be easy to release everything on those six lines, but remember he has nineteen more.

Always look for the simplest, most direct means. Convoluted, intricate pseudopsychiatry will not be useful in acting in these plays. While they bear much examination from a clinical point of view and we can attempt to account for the characters' behaviour in the light of advances in modern research, remember that the fundamental principle contained in these plays, by which the characters behave (and therefore the actors act), is that the action makes sense in the development of the story. Because they are driven figures, influenced by the gods, and because they are searching for an account of their behaviour, they come to terms through the play with why men and women are born, why they do what they do and why they eventually die.

SUMMARY

1. These plays tell a story of universal proportions to provoke the consideration of the great issues regarding man's existence.

2. They are both story and ritual.

3. The chorus is both an actor within the story and a commentator on it and represents the same viewpoint as the audience.

4. The characters embody a universal identity.

5. Do not mistake effort for energy.

6. Identify the changing rhythms, the pulses, of the play.

7. Make the images a sensual experience of the thing or event described.

8. Never reach the ultimate in emotional experience or your technique to express it.

9. Look for the simplest, most direct means.

13
The rules and purpose of playing

HOLDING THE MIRROR UP TO NATURE

Acting, like clothes or hairstyles or speech, changes with fashion in any age. The means by which an actor practises will change according to the times and the development of the form itself. In our current age, we are cautious of dogmas or anything that limits or reduces acting to a formula. It is not appropriate to provide a prescription for the success of an actor. We are aware that we are engaged in an enquiry and that whatever success may be obtained currently will very likely be superseded in the light of future knowledge and opinion. It is with this in mind that I write this book not as the guide book to successful acting, but rather as a contemporary and personal response to what I perceive as the challenges and problems of acting in our theatre today. I am also reminded of two examples of rule-making for the theatre which now seem rather ridiculous and unnecessary.

The first, Goethe's *Rules for Actors*, written in 1803, seem to be dogmatic, though some of them still hold true as principles for consideration:

> First of all, the player must consider that he should not only imitate nature but also portray it ideally, thereby, in his presentation, uniting the true with the beautiful.
>
> Therefore the actor must have complete control over each part of his body so that he may be able to use each limb freely, harmonically, and gracefully, in accord with the expression called for.
>
> The body should be carried in the following manner: the chest up, the upper half of the arms to the elbows somewhat close to the torso, the head slightly turned toward the person to whom one is speaking. But this should be done only slightly so that three quarters of the face is always turned to the audience.
>
> For the actor must always remember that he is on stage for the sake of the audience.
>
> Nor should actors play to each other as if no third person were present. This would be a case of misunderstood naturalness. They

should never act in profile nor turn their backs to the spectators. If it is done in the interests of characterisation or out of necessity, then let it be done with discernment and grace.

One should also take care never to speak in an upstage direction, but always toward the audience. For the actor must always be conscious of two elements, namely, of the person with whom he is engaged in conversation, and of the spectators. Rather than turn the head completely, the eyes should be moved.

It is an important point that when two are acting together, the speaker should always move upstage, while the one who has stopped speaking should move slightly downstage. If this advantageous shifting is carried out with skill – and through practice it can be done with great ease – then the best effect is achieved for the eye as well as for the intelligibility of the declamation. An actor who masters this will produce a very beautiful effect when acting with others who are equally trained. He will have a great advantage over those who do not observe this rule.

It is impossible to imagine an actor today doing anything of this. It is almost directly antithetical to everything we strive for in terms of natural and believable behaviour on stage. Apart from the fact that the specific instructions generalise the approach and the execution of all performances, they directly deny the possibility of a creative individual approach to the art. These rules by reason of their formulaic approach, shift the focus of acting to the execution of technical principles, rather than correspondence with the text and the search for the personality of a character. While we struggle today with the infinite possibility of interpretation, anyone following these rules is obliged to accept a format and a procedure which leads to conformity rather than originality. The examples quoted are only a few of the enormous number of such rules that Goethe wrote, which include intricate direction on almost every aspect of acting, right down to how the fingers should be held.

The second example of such rules was written, somewhat tongue in cheek, by William Oxberry in 1825. He was an actor apparently more noted for his temper and his concerns about his clean shirts than he was for his ability on the stage. His cynical view of acting provides both an insight and a warning:

As the purpose of acting is to obtain, profit, notice and applause, the following Rules are laid down for Histrionics Professors, by following which the *summum bonum* notoriety, (which involves its concomitants) may easily be obtained.

Canons

1. There is no necessity to subject yourself to the slavery of studying your part: – what's the use of the prompter? Besides it's ten to one, that in a modern play, you substitute something from your own mother wit much better than the author wrote. If you are entirely at a loss and out, you will get noticed both by the audience and the critic, which would otherwise, perhaps, have never been the case. As to the feelings of the poet, did he shew any for you, when he put you in the part? And, as he is paid for his play by your master, why mayn't you do what you like with it?

2. Another excellent mode of acquiring notice, is never to be ready to go on the stage, and to have apologies made for you as often as possible.

3. Never attend to another actor in the same scene with you. You may be much better employed in arranging your dress, or in winking and nodding at your friends in the boxes. You must always keep your eye on the benefit.

4. As you take no notice of him, it is very likely he'll take none of you; therefore you may as well, out of respect to the under-standing of your audience, and much better to shew yourself, address all your speeches to the pit, looking them full in the face, and making them quite uneasy in their seats, lest you should expect an answer. This will render you an interesting performer; and you will find judicious persons saying, 'Lord, I do like Mr — ———, you hear every word he says.'

5. If you have any witticism, or good saying to deliver aside, bawl it as loud as you can. How are they to laugh and applaud at the back of the one shilling gallery, if they don't hear what you say? If you have no lungs, give up the profession.

6. Never part with your hat; what are you to do with your fingers?

Oxberry continues with such gems as ignoring other actors during their death scenes and advises actors that the best stance for acting is with one arm extended and the other placed on the hip. 'Other positions are, I know, by some preferred, but take common sense with you, and is it not clear that what is most easily recognised, will be most approved? Then what figure is known better than that of a tea-pot?'

These insights into the serious and satirical attempts to codify the art of acting leave us with many serious decisions to make on the journey towards creating a role without the signposts that formerly existed. The actor has a much greater responsibility to examine and re-examine both his or her craft and art and to render a role believable rather than presentational, real rather than theatrical. We have both the benefit and the curse of hindsight in which time lends perspective to the classical texts but at the same time leaves many matters of behaviour, subject and expression remote. I believe actors of today have to be more literate than they were. The days of 'bare boards and a passion' have passed, and the necessity for sensitive, detailed performance of a play in a world where we compete against the reality of film and the documentation on television of live events as they happen has changed and elevated the expectations for the theatre. No longer is the theatre able to set its own independent conventions and rules; actors have to look at life and, as Shakespeare said so wisely and so prophetically for us, 'hold the mirror up to nature' (*Hamlet*, III.i.22).

Appendix 1
Families, furies, muses and gods

SOME NOTES ON THE MAJOR REFERENCES

A common frustration in working on classical plays is that of not knowing who is who. In the history plays of Shakespeare, sorting out who is the cousin of whom or even which king followed another can be complex. Without a knowledge of the Houses of York and Lancaster it is almost impossible to make complete sense of all that takes place. In the Greek plays not knowing who is related to whom in the House of Atreus or the Theban Dynasty can easily obfuscate what is taking place. For the modern actor, without a traditional classical education, the mysteries of the Furies, the Muses and the Gods are immense. The following are some of the major figures in classical literature of whom one should have some knowledge. The list is not exhaustive, as a glance into any classical dictionary will show.

The Greek Gods

It is generally recognised that fourteen major Gods and Goddesses were represented in Greek mythology (the name for the Roman equivalent is shown in parenthesis):

1. Zeus (Jupiter). The most powerful of the Gods, he was the son of Cronus and Rhea and presided over the sky. He was armed with thunder and lightning, and everything good and evil is ascribable to him.

2. Hera (Juno) was Zeus' sister as well as his queen and wife. There are few stories of her independent of Zeus, but she was the patroness of marriage and of women and was worshipped as the embodiment of earth.

3. Poseidon (Neptune) was generally regarded as having governance of the sea. His home was considered to be deep under the sea, and he is frequently described as riding his chariot over the sea which became calm as he passed. He was a brother of Zeus, though he had less power.

4. Hades (Pluto) was the god of the underworld. He was also a brother of Zeus. He is famous in Greek literature for

carrying off Persephone, the daughter of Demeter. He was relentless and capable of great anger. Because he lived below the earth he was generally believed to endow the earth with crops and minerals.

5. Hestia (Vesta) was a sister of Zeus and ruled over the hearth and home. Both Apollo and Poseidon sued for her hand, and in response she swore to remain a virgin.

6. Hephaestus (Vulcan) was believed to be the son of Hera and possibly Zeus, though some stories say that Hera had him independently of Zeus as a revenge for Zeus having sired Athena independent of her. Hephaestus was born lame, and the story goes that Hera disliked him so much that she flung him from Mount Olympus, where they resided. He is represented as being the smith of the gods and at one time made armour for Achilles.

7. Ares (Mars) was another son of Zeus and Hera. He was the god of war, and because of his unpleasant, savage disposition he was hated by the other gods and by his parents.

8. Apollo (Apollo) was the son of Zeus and Leda. He was supposed to be incredibly handsome and represent all that was best in Greek culture. He is sometimes represented as the god of music and medicine; he also presided over all the arts and over public law and order.

9. Artemis (Diana) was the twin sister of Apollo and the patroness of chastity. She was associated with the moon because of its influence on erotic life. She had care of the young and all births.

10. Demeter (Ceres) was a sister of Zeus and presided over crops and fruits. She was the mother of Persephone, who became the wife of Hades.

11. Aphrodite (Venus) was the Greek goddess of beauty, fertility and love. She fell in love with Ares, in spite of the fact that she was the wife of Hephaestus. She had the ability to confer beauty on mortals.

12. Athena (Minerva), daughter of Zeus and Metis, is often referred to as Pallas Athene. She was the protectress of the Athenian state and personified wisdom. Athena despised love and marriage and was a goddess of war.

13. Hermes (Mercury) was the inventor of the musical instrument the lyre. He was the messenger or herald of the gods and presided over the gifts of eloquence and prudence. He is supposed to have invented many things besides the lyre, including the alphabet.

14. Dionysus (Bacchus) often took the shape of a bull. He was the son of Zeus and Semele. He was the god of the power of nature and of wine and was also regarded as the god of tragic art. He was frequently accompanied by women, and all sorts of orgiastic rites are ascribed to him

The Fates

The three Fates, Clotho, Lachesis and Atropos, sometimes known collectively as Moirae, were often depicted as hideous women. Clotho spun the thread of human life, Lachesis measured its length and Atropos cut it. Sometimes they were regarded as controlling the birth and death of mortals and sometimes they were just allegorical figures representing human life.

The Furies

The Furies were also known as the Eumenides or Erinyes. They were the avenging deities, and in general people were afraid to mention them by their names. They were daughters of the earth or night and are depicted with blood streaming from their eyes, snakes entwined in their hair and bearing wings. Like the Fates, there were three, whose names were Tisiphone, Alecto and Megaera. They were considered to be responsible for punishing man both on earth and afterwards.

The Muses

The Muses were generally held to be the goddesses who presided over music and poetry and over the other arts and sciences. There were nine of them, all daughters of Zeus and Mnemosyne.

They were not worshipped but often invoked, or called on for inspiration.

1. Clio, the Muse of history, who carried a scroll of paper.
2. Euterpe, the Muse of lyric poetry, who carried a flute.
3. Thalia, the Muse of comedy and light poetry, carried the mask of comedy.
4. Melpomene, the Muse of tragedy, who carried a tragic mask.
5. Terpsichore, the Muse of choral dance and songs, who carried a lyre.
6. Erato, the Muse of erotic poetry, who sometimes also carried a lyre.
7. Polyhymnia, a meditative Muse of the sublime hymn.
8. Urania, the Goddess of astronomy, who carried a staff pointing to a globe.
9. Calliope, the Muse of epic poetry, who carried a stylus and a tablet on which to write.

The major houses represented in the Greek drama

In the plays of Euripides, Aeschylus and Sophocles there are several houses that are important. It is imperative to understand who is related to whom in order to understand the stories and to comprehend the tragedy.

The house of Atreus

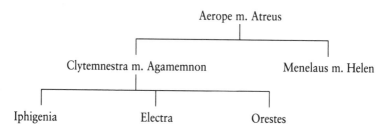

The royal house of Troy

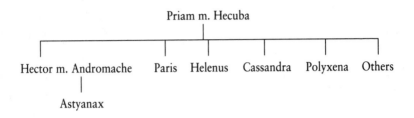

The Theban dynasties

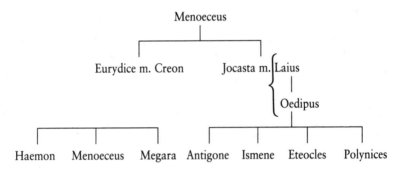

The stories of the individuals in the houses shown above are relayed in the Greek tragedies, and as you read the plays the stories become clearer. The nature of their relationships, beyond that of brother or sister, husband and wife, is often the subject of the plays themselves; we see how families are set against each other or, because of the history of the family, blood feuds are continued.

The humours

The humours are curiosities that are worth noting, since they figured not only in medical beliefs about how the body functioned, but also in philosophical beliefs as to what happened if the mind and spirit were not in accord with nature. Just as there were four elements – earth, air, fire and water – so there were four humours which could cause an imbalance in the body. They each produced an effluence: blood from the heart; yellow bile from the liver, black bile from the spleen and phlegm from the brain. Words such as phlegmatic, splenetic or melancholic, which describe the disposition of a person, were related to the excess or predominance of one of the humours. This is particularly interesting in relation to Hamlet's condition, for example. How much was this human being in control of the humours? Or was his behaviour pre-determined by them? Instead of a therapy session as in our modern day, he would have been offered surgery to let the excessive yellow bile out. Somehow this is much more interesting than a diagnosis in which a modern psychiatrist described the melancholic Dane as 'a bi-polar manic depressive, with rapid cycling'. Great science, I imagine, but not much fun to act. These beliefs were prevalent in early Greek culture and continued in medical practice until the late eighteenth century.

Appendix 2
Chronology of the kings and queens of England and the houses of Lancaster and York

Chronology of the kings and queens of England

1189–99 King Richard I, known as the Lionhearted.

1199–1216 King John, of Magna Carta fame; also the subject of Shakespeare's play of that name.

1216–72 Henry III

1272–1307 Edward I

1307–27 Edward II

1327–77 Edward III

1377–99 Richard II

1399–1413 Henry IV

1413–22 Henry V

1422–61 Henry VI

1461–83 Edward IV

1483 (April 9–June 25) Edward V

1483–85 Richard III

1485–1509 Henry VII

1509–47 Henry VIII

1547–53 Edward VI

1553–58 Mary

1558–1603 Elizabeth I

1603–25 James I

1625–49 Charles I

1649–60 The Commonwealth

1660–85 Charles II

1685–89 James II

1689–94 William III and Mary

1694–1702 William III

1702–14 Anne

1714–27 George I

1727–60 George II

1760–1820 George III

1820–30 George IV

1830–37 William IV

1837–1901 Victoria

1901–10 Edward VII

1910–36 George V

Monarchs and houses in Shakespeare's plays

Below are shown the two houses which are important in understanding Shakespeare's historical plays.

The house of Lancaster

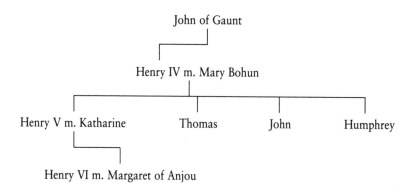

The house of York

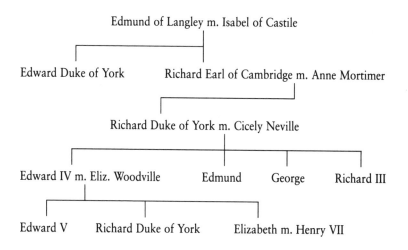

Appendix 3
Duties of household servants

The following extracts are taken from Warne's *Model Cookery and Housekeeping Book*, popular at the turn of the century, which outlined the hierarchical structure of the servants within a household. These descriptions of what was expected of servants would also have applied in the eighteenth and early nineteenth centuries.

The maid of all work

The general servant must be an early riser.

Her first duty, of course, is to open the shutters, and in summer the windows of all the lower part of the house.

Then she must clean the kitchen range and hearth, sifting the cinders, clearing away the ashes, and polishing with a leather the bright parts of the stove, or range.

She must light the fire, fill the kettle, and as soon as the fire burns, set it on to boil.

She must clean the room in which the family breakfast. She must roll up the rug, spread out a coarse piece of canvas before the fireplace, and (if it is winter) she must remove the fender, clean the grate, and light the fire. Then she must just lightly rub over the fire-irons with a leather, replace them, and the fender, and sweep the room over, first pinning up the curtains out of the dust.

She should let the dust settle for a few minutes, running meantime into the kitchen to get the breakfast things ready to bring in.

So it continues: she must sweep everywhere, she must 'put on a large apron and make the beds' and she will be the last to bed because she 'will carefully fasten the house'. She is told that 'Her hair should be banded carefully back, and be kept smooth, and her face clean; and as she has to answer the door, she should wear her coarse apron as much as possible, and at a knock or ring exchange it for a clean white one.'

The footman

Where there is no butler kept he brings in the breakfast urn, and afterwards removes the breakfast things. The footman lays the luncheon cloth and dinner cloth, and waits table.

The footman brings in letters and notes; he must always hand them on a waiter [a salver or tray]. He must answer bells readily, especially the door-bell, and he should speak civilly to visitors. He shows them in, asks the name if he does not know it, and takes care to announce them properly.

The valet

The valet's duty is to wait on his master.

He sees that the gentleman's dressing-room fire is lighted in the morning; arranges the clothes, which he has brushed, on a table or chair, and places the linen before the fire. Then he fills the bath, &c. Sometimes the valet shaves his master; he brushes his hair, and should be able to cut it every fortnight. He hands the garments required to the gentleman.

The butler

The butler is at the head of the men servants; he has care of the plate and wine. He supervises all meals and shares duties answering the door and announcing visitors with the under-butler and footman.

The lady's-maid

A lady's-maid is required to be a nice mannered, respectable-looking young woman; she should be a tolerably good dress-maker; know how to make a cap or trim a bonnet; and she must be a good hair dresser. Her first morning duty will be to dress her lady, about which it is impossible to give directions, as ladies differ very much in their toilette arrangements . . .

A good deal of sitting up at night is sometimes required from a lady's-maid during the London season; she must strive to get what rest she can, and good-temperedly support any inevitable fatigue.

A cheerful, kindly performance of her duties, deference, obedience, industry, and strict honesty will secure for her a friend in her lady, and a happy home under all ordinary circumstances.

Bibliography

Acting

Building a Character, Constantin Stanislavski, Translated by
   Elizabeth Reynolds Hapgood, Theatre Arts Books
Acting Skills, Hugh Morrison, Black/Theatre Arts
To the Actor, Michael Chekhov, Harper and Row
Respect for Acting, Uta Hagen, Macmillan
Acting in Restoration Comedy, Simon Callow, Applause
   Theatre Books

Voice and Speech

Voice and Speech in the Theatre, Clifford Turner, A & C Black
Clear Speech, Malcolm Morrison, A & C Black
Voice and the Actor, Cicely Berry, Virgin Books
Training the Speaking Voice, Virgil Anderson, Oxford
   University Press

Shakespeare

Prefaces to Shakespeare, Harley Granville Barker, Batsford
What Happens in Hamlet, John Dover Wilson, Cambridge
   University Press

General

The Oxford Companion to the Theatre, Oxford University Press
English Pronouncing Dictionary, Daniel Jones, Cambridge
   University Press
Everyman's Smaller Classical Dictionary, Dent
Classical Mythology, Mark P.O. Morford and Robert J. Lenardon,
   Longman
A Source Book in Theatrical History, A.M. Nagler, Dover
On the Art of the Theatre, Edward Gordon Craig,
   Mercury Books

The Story of English, Robert McCrum, William Cran, Robert MacNeil, Penguin

Form and Meaning in Drama, H.D.F. Kitto, University Paperbacks

The Greeks, H.D.F. Kitto, Penguin

The Polite World, Joan Wildeblood and Peter Brinson, Oxford University Press

The Shakespeare quotations are taken from *The Complete Oxford Shakespeare*, edited by Stanley Wells and Gary Taylor, Oxford University Press (1988).

Index